# Dancing on the Whirlwind

# 소용돌이 속에서 춤을

## 소용돌이 속에서 춤을

대행큰스님 법문
생활 속의 참선수행 *17* / 한영합본

| | |
|---|---|
| 발행일 | 2019년 8월 초판1쇄 |
| 영문번역 | 한마음국제문화원 |
| 표지디자인 | 박수연 |
| 편집 | 한마음국제문화원 |
| 발행 | 한마음출판사 |
| 출판등록 | 384-2000-000010 |
| 전화 | 031-470-3175 |
| 팩스 | 031-470-3209 |
| 이메일 | onemind@hanmaum.org |

### *Dancing on the Whirlwind*

Practice in Daily Life *17* / Bilingual, Korean · English
Dharma Talks by Seon Master Daehaeng

First Edition, First Printing: August 2019
English Translation by
Hanmaum International Culture Institute
Edited by Hanmaum International Culture Institute
Cover Design by Su Yeon Park
Published by Hanmaum Publications
www.hanmaumbooks.org

Printed in the Republic of Korea

ISBN 978-89-91857-57-5 (04220) / 978-89-91857-50-6 (set)

이 도서의 국립중앙도서관 출판예정도서목록(CIP)은 서지정보
유통지원시스템 홈페이지(http://seoji.nl.go.kr)와 국가자료종합
목록 구축시스템(http://kolis-net.nl.go.kr)에서 이용하실 수 있
습니다. (CIP제어번호 : CIP2019028720)

# Dancing on the Whirlwind

Seon Master Daehaeng

# 소용돌이 속에서 춤을

대행큰스님 법문

hanmaum

# 차 례

# CONTENTS

# 대우주를 걷는 길

다가오는 모든 걸 한 곳에 맡겨놓고

안 되는 건 되게끔 돌려놓고,

매사를 다 그렇게 하셔야 합니다.

어떠한 게 속에서 일어나고 일어나도

또 바깥에서 부닥치고 부닥쳐 오더라도

모든 것은 참나인 근본에서

어찌하고 어찌하나 보려는 것입니다.

Stepping Forward into the Great Sky

Entrust everything that confronts you to one place.
Even when things don't go well,
return them to the one place
with this intention,
"Make this work out for the best,
work out for the best."
Return everything in this way.
Even when something arises again and again from inside,
or confronts you continuously from the outside,
all of this is your true self,
your foundation,
testing you,
checking you,
seeing how you handle things.

내 힘에 넘치는 일이 다가온다 하더라도

겁내지 말고, 싫다 좋다 생각 말고

모든 일이 내 일이다 생각하고 가십시오.

상대를 부드럽고 부드럽게 대하고

또 말도 부드럽고 부드럽게 하고

모든 걸 지혜로운 한마음에 놓아 간다면

비로소 내가 있는 소식이 오게 됩니다.

보이지 않는 근본에 모두 굴려 놓으면

내 안의 불이 켜지게 됩니다.


-대행큰스님 게송 중에서

Even when things overwhelm you,
don't be scared,
don't get caught up in like and dislike.
Just take it all as a part of your life,
as part of your practice.
So respond to others gently, gently,
speak to others gently, gently,
let go of everything to this wise one mind.

When you can do this,
one day news of your true self will come.
When you return everything to your unseen foundation,
one day a great light will arise within you.

—Daehaeng Kun Sunim

## 머리글

대행큰스님이 지난 50여 년 동안 끊임없이 중생들에게 베풀어 주신 수많은 법문이 있었지만, 핵심을 짚어 내는 하나의 단어가 있다면, 그건 아마도 "참나"일 것입니다. 항상 나와 함께 있어서 보지 못하는 내 안의 진짜 나, 그 "참나"를 발견하여 당당하고 싱그럽게 살아가기를 바라는, 중생을 위한 스님의 간절한 바람은 이 한 편의 법문 속에도 여지없이 드러나 있습니다.

누구에게나 내면에는 만물만생을 다 먹여 살리고도 되남는 마음속 한 점의 불씨가 있습니다. 그 영원한 불씨를 찾아 광대무변한 마음법의 이치를 체득하여, 진정한 자유인으로서, 우주의 한 일원으로서 당당히 그 역할을 해나가길 바라는 대행큰스님의 간곡한 뜻이 이 법문을 통해 여러분 모두의 마음에 전해지길 바랍니다.

한마음국제문화원 일동 합장

## Foreword

Over the last fifty years, Daehaeng Kun Sunim gave countless Dharma talks and teachings to beings without number, but if all those talks could be summed up into one word, it would be "true self."

This true essence has always been with us, yet remains unseen. Discover it for yourself, and in doing so, learn to live with courage, dignity, and joy. That all beings should awaken to this true essence is Daehaeng Kun Sunim's deepest wish. When you've tasted the most refreshing spring water imaginable, you naturally want to share it with others.

Within us all is this seed, this spark that feeds and sustains each and every being. Discover this eternal spark and realize its profound and unlimited ability. If you can do this, you'll know what it means to truly be a free person, and you can fulfill the great role that is yours as a member of the whole universe.

With palms together,
The Hanmaum International Culture Institute

## 대행큰스님에 대하여

대행큰스님께서는 여러 면에서 매우 보기 드문 선사(禪師)셨다. 무엇보다 선사라면 당연히 비구 스님을 떠올리는 전통 속에서 여성으로서 선사가 되셨으며, 비구 스님들을 제자로 두었던 유일한 비구니 스님이셨고, 노년층 여성이 주된 신도계층을 이루었던 한국 불교에 젊은 세대의 청장년층 남녀들을 대거 참여하게 만들어 한국불교에 새로운 풍격(風格)을 일으키는 데 일조한 큰 스승이셨다. 또한 전통 비구니 강원과 비구니 종단에 대한 지속적인 지원을 펼치심으로써 비구니 승단을 발전시키는데 중추적인 역할을 하셨다.

큰스님께서는 어느 누구나 마음수행을 통해 깨달을 수 있음을 강조하시면서 삭발제자와 유발제자를 가리지 않고 법을 구하는 이들에게는 모두 똑같이 가르침을 주셨다.

## About Daehaeng Kun Sunim

Daehaeng *Kun Sunim*[1](1927 – 2012) was a rare teacher in Korea: a female *Seon*(Zen)[2] master, a nun whose students also included monks, and a teacher who helped revitalize Korean Buddhism by dramatically increasing the participation of young people and men.

She broke out of traditional models of spiritual practice to teach in such a way that allowed anyone to practice and awaken, making laypeople a particular focus of her efforts. At

---

**1. Sunim / Kun Sunim:** Sunim is the respectful title of address for a Buddhist monk or nun in Korea, and Kun Sunim is the title given to outstanding nuns or monks.

**2. Seon**(禪)(Chan, Zen): Seon describes the unshakeable state where one has firm faith in their inherent foundation, their Buddha-nature, and so returns everything they encounter back to this fundamental mind. It also means letting go of "I," "me," and "mine" throughout one's daily life.

스님은 1927년 서울에서 태어나 일찍이 9세경에 자성을 밝히셨고 당신이 증득(證得)하신 바를 완성하기 위해 오랫동안 산중에서 수행하셨다. 훗날, 누더기가 다 된 해진 옷을 걸치고 손에 주어지는 것만을 먹으며 지냈던 그 당시를 회상하며 스님은 의도적으로 고행을 하고자 했던 것이 아니라 당신에게 주어진 환경이 그러했노라고, 또한 근본 불성자리에 일체를 맡기고 그 맡긴 일이 어떻게 작용하는지를 관하는 일에 완전히 몰두하고 있었기에 다른 것에는 신경을 쓸 틈이 없었노라고 말씀하셨다.

그 시절의 체험이 스님의 가르치는 방식을 형성하는 데 깊은 영향을 미쳤다. 스님은 우리가 본래부터 어마어마한 잠재력을, 무궁무진한 에너지와 지혜를 가지고 있는데도 대부분이 그 역량을 알지 못해 끊임없이 많은 고통을 겪으며 살고 있음을 절실히 느끼며 안타까워하셨다. 우리들 각자 안에 존재하는 이 위대한 빛을 명백히 알고 있었기에, 스님은 본래부터 가지고 있는 근본자성(自性)인 '참나'를 믿고 의지해 살라 가르치셨고, 이 중요한 진리에서 벗어나는 그 어떤 것도 가르치기를 단호히 거부하셨다.

the same time, she was a major force for the advancement of *Bhikkunis*,[3] heavily supporting traditional nuns' colleges as well as the modern Bhikkuni Council of Korea.

Born in Seoul, Korea, she awakened when she was around eight years old and spent the years that followed learning to put her understanding into practice. For years, she wandered the mountains of Korea, wearing ragged clothes and eating only what was at hand. Later, she explained that she hadn't been pursuing some type of asceticism; rather, she was just completely absorbed in entrusting everything to her fundamental *Buddha*[4] essence and observing how that affected her life.

---

**3. Bhikkunis:** Female sunims who are fully ordained are called *Bhikkuni* (比丘尼) sunims, while male sunims who are fully ordained are called *Bhikku* (比丘) sunims. This can also be a polite way of indicating male or female sunims.

**4. Buddha:** In this text, "Buddha" is capitalized out of respect, because it represents the essence and function of the enlightened mind. "The Buddha" always refers to Sakyamuni Buddha.

의도한 바는 아니셨지만, 스님은 매일매일의 일상 속에서 누구나 내면에 갖추어 가지고 있는 근본이자 진수(眞髓)인 참나와 진정으로 통할 수 있게 되었을 때 어떠한 일이 일어나는지를 역력히 보여 주셨다. 사람들은 스님 곁에 있을 때 자신들을 무한히 받아 주고 품어 주는 것만 같은, 말로 형언키 어려운 정밀(靜謐)한 기운을 느꼈고, 스님이 다른 사람들을 도와줄 때 드러내 보이는 깊은 법력 또한 목도하곤 하였다. 하지만 이 모든 일들은 당신 자신을 돋보이게 하거나 과시하려 했던 게 아니었다. 사실 스님께서는 당신의 법력을 늘 감추려고 하셨다. 마음공부의 목적이 놀라운 능력을 갖게 되는 것이 아님에도 대중들이 그것에만 집착하게 되는 폐단을 우려하셨기 때문이었다.

그렇지만 당신이 하신 모든 일을 통해, 우리가 내면에 있는 근본과 진정으로 하나가 되었을 때 그 능력과 자유로움이 어떤 것인지를 보여주셨다. 스님은 우리 모두가 근본을 통해 연결되어 있으므로 다 통할 수 있고, 그럼으로써 서로 깊이 이해할 수 있다는 것을 보여 주셨으며, 더 나아가 우리가 근본

Those years profoundly shaped Kun Sunim's later teaching style; she intimately knew the great potential, energy, and wisdom inherent within each of us, and recognized that most of the people she encountered suffered because they didn't realize this about themselves. Seeing clearly the great light in every individual, she taught people to rely upon this inherent foundation, and refused to teach anything that distracted from this most important truth.

Without any particular intention to do so, Daehaeng Kun Sunim demonstrated on a daily basis the freedom and ability that arise when we truly connect with this fundamental essence inherent within us.

The sense of acceptance and connection people felt from being around her, as well as the abilities she manifested, weren't things she was trying to show off. In fact, she usually tried to hide them because people would tend to cling to these, without realizing that chasing after them cannot lead to either freedom or awakening.

자리에서 일으키는 한생각이 이 세상에 법이 되어 돌아갈 수 있다는 것도 보여 주셨다.

어떤 의미에서는 이 모든 일이 우리가 만물만생과 정말로 하나가 되었을 때 자연스레 부수적으로 나오는 것이라고 할 수 있다. 상대를 둘로 보거나 방해물로 여기는 마음이 사라졌을 때, 진정으로 모두와 조화롭게 흘러갈 수 있게 되었을 때 이 모든 일이 가능할 수 있게 되는 것이다. 이렇게 되면, 다가오는 상대가 누구든 별개의 존재로 느끼지 않게 된다. 그들이 또 다른 우리 자신들의 모습이기 때문이다. 일체가 둘이 아님을 뼛속 깊이 느끼는 사람이, 어찌 자신 앞에 닥친 인연을 나 몰라라 하고 등져 버릴 수 있겠는가?

스님은 중생들이 가지고 오는 어려운 문제나 상황들을 해결할 수 있도록 도와주셨으며, 이러한 스님의 자비로운 원력은 당신이 도시로 나와 본격적으로 대중들을 가르치기 이전에 이미 한국에서는 전설이 되어 있었다. 1950년대 말경, 치악산 상원사 근처 한 움막에서 수행차 몇 년간 머무르신 적이 있었는데, 그 소문을 듣고 전국에서 찾아오는 사람

Nonetheless, in her very life, in everything she did, she was an example of the true freedom and wisdom that arise from this very basic, fundamental essence that we all have – that we are. She showed that because we are all interconnected, we can deeply understand what's going on with others, and that the intentions we give rise to can manifest and function in the world.

All of these are, in a sense, side effects, things that arise naturally when we are truly one with everyone and everything around us. They happen because we are able to flow in harmony with our world, with no dualistic views or attachments to get in the way. At this point, other beings are not cut off from us; they are another aspect of ourselves. Who, feeling this to their very bones, could turn their back on others?

It was this deep compassion that made her a legend in Korea long before she formally started teaching. She was known for having the spiritual power to help people in all circumstances and with every kind of problem. She compared compassion to freeing a fish from a drying

들이 끊이질 않았다. 차마 그들의 고통스러운 호소를 내칠 수가 없었던 스님은 일일이 그들의 말에 귀 기울이며 마음을 다해 그들을 도와주셨다. 스님은 자비를 물 마른 웅덩이에서 죽어 가는 물고기를 살리는 방생에 비유하셨다. 집세가 없어 셋집에서 쫓겨난 사람들에게 집을 마련해 주고, 학비가 없어서 학교를 마칠 수 없는 학생들에게 학비를 대주셨지만, 스님의 자비행(慈悲行)을 아는 사람은 손에 꼽을 정도밖에 되지 않았다.

그러나 문제를 해결해 주면 그때뿐 또 다른 문제가 닥쳐오면 속수무책이 되어 버리고 마는 사람들을 보며, 스님께서는 중생들이 자신의 문제를 스스로 해결하고 **윤회(輪廻)**[1]의 굴레에서 벗어나 자유인이 될 수 있는 도리를 가르치는 일이 더 시급함을 느끼셨다. 누구나가 다 가지고 있는 '참나', 이 내면의 밝디밝은 진수(眞髓)를 알게 하여, 자신들이

---

**1. 윤회(輪廻):** 산스크리트의 삼사라(samsara)를 번역한 말로 쉼 없이 돈다는 생사의 바퀴를 뜻함. 다시 말해, 수레바퀴가 끊임없이 구르는 것과 같이, 중생이 번뇌와 업에 의하여 삼계(三界: 색계, 욕계, 무색계) 육도(六道: 지옥, 아귀, 축생, 아수라, 인간, 천상)라는 생사의 세계를 그치지 않고 돌고 도는 현상을 일컬음.

puddle, putting a homeless family into a home, or providing the school fees that would allow a student to finish high school. And when she did things like this, and more, few knew that she was behind it.

Her compassion was also unconditional. She would offer what help she could to individuals and organizations, whether they be Christian or Buddhist, a private organization or governmental. She would help nuns' temples that had no relationship with her temple, Christian organizations that looked after children living on their own, city-run projects to help care for the elderly, and much, much more. Yet, even when she provided material support, always there was the deep, unseen aid she offered through this connection we all share.

However, she saw that ultimately, for people to live freely and go forward in the world as a blessing to all around them, they needed to know about this bright essence that is within each of us.

자유롭게 사는 것은 물론이요, 자신들의 삶이 인연 맺은 모든 이에게 축복이 되어 이 한세상을 활달히 살아갈 수 있도록 해야겠다고 다짐하셨다.

마침내 산에서 내려온 스님께서는 1972년 경기도 안양에 한마음선원을 설립하셨다. 이후 40여 년 동안 한마음선원에 주석하시며, 지혜를 원하는 자에게 지혜를, 배고프고 가난한 자에게는 먹을 것과 물질을, 아파하는 자에게는 치유의 방편을 내어 주시는 무한량의 자비를 베푸시며 불법의 진리를 가르쳐 주셨다. 스님은 도움이 필요한 다양한 사회복지 프로그램을 후원하셨고, 6개국에 10개의 국외 지원과 국내 15개의 지원을 세우셨다. 또한 스님의 가르침은 영어, 독어, 스페인어, 러시아어, 중국어, 일본어, 불어, 이태리어, 베트남어, 체코어, 인도네시아어 등으로 번역 출간되었다. 스님은 2012년 5월 22일 0시, 세납 86세로 입적하셨으며, 법랍 63세셨다.

To help people discover this for themselves, she founded the first *Hanmaum*[5] Seon Center in 1972. For the next forty years she gave wisdom to those who needed wisdom, food and money to those who were poor and hungry, and compassion to those who were hurting.

---

**5. Hanmaum**[han-ma-um]: *Han* means one, great, and combined, while *maum* means mind, as well as heart, and together they mean everything combined and connected as one.

What is called *Hanmaum* is intangible, unseen, and transcends time and space. It has no beginning or end, and is sometimes called our fundamental mind. It also means the mind of all beings and everything in the universe connected and working together as one. In English, we usually translate this as *one mind*.

본 저서는 대행큰스님의 법문을
한국어와 영어 합본 시리즈로 출간하는
〈생활 속의 참선수행〉시리즈 제17권으로
1996년 6월 16일 정기법회 때 설하신 내용을
재편집한 것입니다. 몇 개의 질문은 다른 법문에서
발췌해 추가하였습니다.

This Dharma talk was given by
Daehaeng Kun Sunim on Sunday, June 16, 1996,
with some related questions added from other talks.
This is Volume 17 in the ongoing series,
*Practice in Daily Life*.

Daehaeng Kun Sunim founded ten overseas
branches of Hanmaum Seon Center, and her
teachings have been translated into twelve
different languages to date: English, German,
Russian, Chinese, French, Spanish, Indonesian,
Italian, Japanese, Vietnamese, Estonian, and
Czech, in addition to the original Korean. For more
information about these or the overseas centers,
please see the back of this book.

# 소용돌이 속에서 춤을

1996년 6월 16일

### 불붙은 집 속에 내가 있다면

오늘, 날도 궂고 이 도량도 좁은데 이렇게 같이 한자리를 하게 돼서 감사합니다. 지난번에도 얘기했듯이 우리 인생살이가 상당히 복잡하고, 또 살얼음판 위를 걷는 것과 같아 마구 살면 안 됩니다. 화를 낸다는 건 살얼음판 위에 모닥불을 지피는 것과 같아서, 그런 일이 계속되면 얼음이 깨져버려, 내가 빠진단 말입니다.

그런데도 그걸 모르고 언제 깨질지 모르는 이 살얼음판과 같은 인생을 하루라도 빨리 벗어나야 되는데 이러니저러니 탓을 하고 간섭을 하면서 화를 내며 갑니다. 이러니까 자기 갈 길을 못 가고, 때에 따라서는 얼음이 깨져 빠지게 되는 거죠.

# Dancing on the Whirlwind

June 16, 1996

## Escaping from a Burning House

Thank you so much for gathering together like this in spite of the bad weather and crowded space. As I mentioned last time, this daily life of ours is like walking on a frozen lake, all the while trying to juggle a hundred different things. And the ice is thin. Very thin. Would you stop and build a campfire on such ice? No. But that's what happens when we get angry.

People don't realize just how thin the ice is, yet they build a fire there and keep feeding it with anger, blame, resentment, and attempts to dominate and control others. How soon before the ice gives way? How long before they're left flailing and struggling, trying to escape the freezing water? They certainly won't be taking any more steps forward on their own path.

예를 들어 여러분이 있는 빌딩에 큰불이 났다고 칩시다. 그러면 아마 나갈 방법부터 찾을 겁니다. 그 생각이 우선이지 다른 거는 차후의 문제죠. 이 부처님 법을 공부하는 것도 역시 그렇게 해야 한다는 얘깁니다.

저는 이날까지 오직 내 근본자리만을 믿고 일체를 거기에 맡겨 놓아 이 공기주머니에서 벗어나 자유자재로 사는 거, 그거였습니다. 사실 건강, 돈, 먹는 거, 잘 사는 거 다 중요한 거지만, 이런 거 저런 거 상관 안 하고 어떻게 이 중요한 사실을 알려 줘야 하나 오직 그거뿐이었습니다. 지금도 그렇고요. 그 부분은 아마 세세생생에 변치 않을 겁니다.

For example, suppose this building was on fire. Finding a way out would be the only thing on your mind. Every other problem would be forgotten. Learning how to rely upon your *fundamental mind*[6] and free yourself is exactly this urgent.

Learning how to become truly free is the only thing I've ever paid attention to. Ever since I was little, all my focus was on going forward while entrusting everything to this fundamental mind, and learning how I could be free from the bonds of this *middle realm*.[7] Health, money, eating well,

---

**6. Fundamental mind:** This refers to our inherent essence, that which we fundamentally are. "Mind," in Mahayana Buddhism, almost never means the brain or intellect. Instead it refers to this essence, through which we are inherently connected to everything, everywhere. It is intangible, beyond space and time, and has no beginning or end. It is the source of everything, and everyone is endowed with it. "Fundamental Mind" is interchangeable with other terms such as "Buddha-nature," "True nature," "True self," and "Foundation."

**7. Middle realm(world):** In Buddhism, the realm of human beings is sometimes described as the "middle realm" or the "middle world," because it said to be one of six realms. It exists below the realms of more advanced beings, called devas and asuras, but above the realms of animals, hungry ghosts, and the various hell states.

석가모니 부처님께서는 예전에 이미 우리가 인생을 어떻게 살아야 하는지 그 길을 제시해 주셨습니다. 말씀하시길 "공(空)이 **색(色)²**이고 색이 공이니라. 그러하니 그대로 **여여(如如)³**하니라."라고 하셨습니다. 그런데 사람들은 그 뜻을 헤아리질 못합니다.

---

**2. 색(色)**: 눈에 보이는 현상세계, 즉 물질세계를 일컬음.

**3. 여여(如如)**: 만물만생이 평등하고 차별 없이 어디에도 머물지 않고 끊임없이 흘러 돌아가고 있는 그대로의 모습. 일체가 고정됨이 없이 돌아가는 진실의 모습을 말하며, 이러한 진리의 흐름에 부합하는 삶을 살아가는 것을 여여한 삶이라 함.

living comfortably – these aren't unimportant, but I have no interest in them. What truly matters is helping people understand how they can free themselves. This is all I've paid attention to and all I'll ever do. Learning how to free yourself is the most urgent thing any of us can do.

Sakyamuni *Buddha*[8] showed us how we should live when he said, "*Form*[9] is *emptiness*,[10] and emptiness is form. Thus, everything is already flowing naturally and freely." However, people don't fully realize the implications of this.

---

**8. Buddha:** In this text, "Buddha" and "Bodhisattva" are capitalized out of respect, because these represent the essence and function of the enlightened mind. "The Buddha" always refers to Sakyamuni Buddha.

**9. Form:** In Korean, the Sino-Korean character for form (色) also includes things like emotions, evaluations, and views. It can be described as the material world and the experiences, emotions, and thoughts arising from the interactions taking place within it.

**10. Emptiness:** Emptiness is not a void, but rather refers to the ceaseless flowing of all things. Everything is flowing as part of one whole, so there is nothing that can be separated out and set aside as if it existed independently of everything else. There is, therefore, no "me" that exists apart from other people or other things. There is only the interpenetrated and interdependent whole, "empty" of any independent or separate selves or objects.

**마음**[4]은 체가 없어 광대무변하고 영묘(靈妙)하니까 이 육통(肉桶)을 벗어나, 공기주머니 안에서 벗어나라고 하신 건데 사람들은 영 그 뜻을 헤아리질 못합니다.

### 일체가 흐르는데 붙들 게 있을까?

가끔 제가 이런 말을 하지요? "업(業)이 없는 거다." "고(苦)가 없다." 이런 말이에요. 하지만 우리 삶이 그렇지 않은데, 그럼 무슨 까닭에 없다고 하는 걸까요?

여러분이 가정에서는 아버지가 됐다가, 남편이 됐다가, 또 밖에서는 다른 역할을 합니다. 평상시에 살아가시면서 보고 듣고, 말하고 만나고, 가고 오고 하는 이 모든 게 이렇게 다단하게 바뀌면서 지나갑니다. 뭘 하더라도 모든 게 훅훅 그냥 날아갑니다.

---

**4. 마음**: 단순히 두뇌를 통한 정신활동이나 지성을 일컫는 말이 아니라, 만물만생이 지니고 있으며, 일체만법을 움직이게 하는 천지의 근본을 뜻함. '안에 있다, 밖에 있다' 혹은, '이거다 저거다'라고 말할 수 없으며 시작과 끝이 없고 사라질 수도 파괴될 수도 없음. 시공을 초월하여 존재함.

Sakyamuni Buddha was telling us that our mind is utterly limitless, unhindered by anything, and unfathomably mysterious. This mind of ours is utterly free of all fixed forms, so if we use our minds wisely, we can be free from the limitations of this sack of flesh. We can be free from this bubble of air we're trapped in, this middle realm.[11]

### Everything is Flowing, So What's There to Carry With You?

Sometimes I say things like, "There is no such thing as karma," or "There is no suffering." However, we experience both of these, don't we? So why do I say they don't exist? Because everything keeps flowing without ceasing.

When you're at home, sometimes you're a father, sometimes you become a husband, and then you're someone else when you go to work. Everything you experience in life is ceaselessly changing like this – what you see, what you hear,

---

11. "Bubble of air" and "middle realm" refer, respectively, to the Earth and the material world as we normally perceive it.

사실 날아간다는 단어도 붙질 않아야 되겠죠? 하지만 말을 하려니까 그렇습니다.

여기 올라오실 때도 뒷발자국 자체가 그냥 휙휙 가버렸죠? 하나 떼어 놓은 사이에 벌써 하나가 가버리고, 하나 떼어 놓은 사이에 가버리고 말입니다.

보는 것도 그렇고 듣는 것도 그렇습니다. 모든 게 이렇게 스치듯, 흘러가듯 연방 자연스레 가버리는 걸 어떻게 생각하십니까?

그런데 말입니다, 이거 잘 들으십시오. 여러분 중에는 물론 상근기가 있고 중근기가 있고 하근기가 있겠죠. 하지만 근기대로 모아 놓고 말을 할 수는 없으니, 지금 내가 하는 소리를 듣고, 여러분들이 알아서 잘하십시오. 여러분의 차원에서 더 높은 근기로 튀어 올라가려면, 이 소리를 듣고 튀어 올라가 벗어나란 얘깁니다.

what you say, where you go – all of it just flies by. Even the words "flies by" can't adequately describe this. Yet I have to use some kind of words to convey a sense of this.

When you came up to the *Dharma*[12] Hall today, you just walked up, taking one step after another, right? You didn't try to cling to each footstep, did you? Each time you lifted your foot, that previous footstep disappeared as if it had never happened. It's there and gone in an instant, with nothing in it to cling to.

Everything you see, hear, and experience is like this. It's all just brushing past us, flowing naturally. From the very beginning it's flowed like this, without cease. Think about what this means for your life.

People actually do have different levels of spirituality. There are some people who are very deep, others who are quite shallow, and the rest are somewhere in between. Even here today, some people can easily follow me, while others have a hard time. But these levels aren't fixed things;

---

**12. Dharma:** This refers to both ultimate truth, and the truth taught by the Buddha.

앞에 얘기한 것처럼, 보는 것도 듣는 것도, 가고 오는 것도, 몸을 움죽거리는 것도, 누굴 만나는 것도 그냥 흘러가는 거기 때문에, 어느 시점에, 혹은 무언가를 고정해 놓을 수가 없어요. 그렇게 고정시켜 놓을 수가 없는데, 어떻게 "내가 했다"라고 할 수 있습니까?

어떤 거 할 때 내가 움죽거렸다고 할 거며, 어떤 거 봤을 때 내가 봤다고 할 거며, 어떤 걸 들었을 때 내가 들었다고 할 겁니까? 그래서 고도 업도 붙을 사이가 없는 거예요. 붙을 자리가 없는 게 아니라, 그럴 사이가 없다고요.

they aren't permanent states. If you want to raise your level, then listen carefully to what I'm going to say and try to apply it. Work hard at it and jump!

Please listen carefully: Not a single thing is fixed and unchanging. Nothing you see, hear, or do remains the same. The moment you meet someone, the instant you arrive somewhere, it all flows away and is gone. There's nothing to grab hold of, so what is there that you would claim as something "I did"?

Both the "I" of that moment, as well as all the things "I did," are already gone. All the things that "I saw," as well as the "me" who saw them, have vanished. The "me" who was there listening, as well as everything "I heard" are gone. There's no instant in which karma or suffering could stick to you. Even here, it's not an issue of there being some place for these things to stick to, it's that there's no instant for any of that to happen. There's no moment for karma, suffering, or happiness to stick to anything. Let alone any place where they could stick.

You and everything you see flies by in an instant. You, the person who's hearing, as well as

보고는 훌떡 가고, 듣고는 훌떡 가고, 움죽거리
곤 훌떡 가고, 만나고 훌떡 가고, 하고 훌떡 가고
이러는데, 붙을 사이가 있어야 붙을 거 아닙니까?
그럴 사이가 없으니 붙을 자리도 없겠죠.

그럼에도 불구하고, 이것 보고 말들 하고, 저것
보고 말들 하고, 이거 듣고 말하고 저거 듣고 말하
고, 말들이 많아요. 흘러가는 대로 두질 않고, 본
거에 대해, 들은 거에 대해 말이 많죠. 말을 하지
말라는 건 아닌데, 말을 하되 분별없이 하나로 여여
하게 돌아가는 이 도리를 알고, 함이 없이 하라 이
겁니다.

그래야 고가 되거나 업이 되지 않는 겁니다. 이
도리를 알면 함이 없이 하는 것이 됩니다. 함이 없
이 사랑하고, 함이 없이 보시하고, 함이 없이 듣고,
함이 없이 책도 보고 공부하라 이겁니다.

what you hear, what you do, what you feel, the people you encounter – all are there and gone. And there's certainly no instant when something could be stuck to something else.

Nonetheless, people see something and then talk and talk about it. They hear something, and talk and talk about it. At the drop of a hat, they give rise to so many opinions and judgements. It all wants to flow, but they won't let it. I'm not saying that it's bad to talk and think about things, but you also need to be aware that everything is flowing and circulating as one, naturally. So when you speak, do it while letting go of any traces of "I," as well as any judgements or discriminations.

When you're truly aware of how everything is flowing and working together as one whole, then whatever you do will naturally be free of any trace of discrimination or distinction between "you" and "others." Thus, the things you do and say won't end up creating more karma or suffering. So love others, but do it unconditionally. Listen to others, but do it while letting go of any traces of "I." Learn and study, but do it while letting go of any thoughts of "I know."

이런 말을 하는 까닭은 여러분이 이 도리를 알고 행하면서 생활하면, 인간 세상에서 산다 해도, 인간 세상이 아닌 인간 세상에서 살게 되는 거라 그렇습니다. 즉, 유(有)의 세계에서 모든 용무를 하면서 모든 것을 돌볼 수 있단 말입니다.

The reason I'm telling you this is that if you understand how everything works together as one through this fundamental mind of ours, and go forward trying to apply this truth to your daily life, then even though you continue to live in this world, you'll be able to function far above the human realm. In other words, while taking care of all your ordinary responsibilities in this material realm, you can also work through the unseen realm to help with problems, both seen and unseen, around the world.

If you work diligently at trying to apply this fundamental mind to your daily life, then you will be able to guide all of the *karmic consciousnesses*[13]

---

**13. Karmic consciousnesses**(業識)**:** Our thoughts, feelings, and behaviors are recorded as the consciousnesses of the lives that make up our body. These are sometimes called karmic consciousnesses, although they don't have independent awareness or volition. Sometime afterwards, these consciousnesses will come back out. Thus we may feel happy, sad, angry, etc., without an obvious reason, or they may cause other problems to occur. The way to dissolve these consciousnesses is not to react to them when they arise, and instead to entrust them to our foundation. However, even these consciousnesses are just temporary combinations, so we shouldn't cling to the concept of them.

세세생생의 모든 것을 이끌고 가면서, 지금 현재 세상도 버리지 않고, 현재 몸도 버리지 않고, 현재 생활도 버리지 않으면서도, 모든 것을 다 버리는 게 되는 거고, 그래서 모든 것을 다 얻을 수가 있게 되는 겁니다. 그리고 얻은 것을 다 베풀어 줄 수 있게끔 만드십시오.

## 마음 기둥 하나만을 꽉 쥐고 여여히 돌아가기

여러분은 겉모습을 보고 말을 듣고 평가를 하는 데 그렇게 고정되게 마음을 쓰면 안 됩니다. 예를 들어 석가모니 부처님께서는 때에 따라 벌레를 위해 벌레가 되기도 했습니다. 벌레가 저항력을 느끼지 않게 하려고, 벌레 마음이 되어 들어가는 것입니다.

within you, as well as those beings you've created *karmic affinity*[14] with as you've passed through life after life. And you'll be able to do this while being present in the world, taking care of your body, and taking care of the people and things that are part of your ordinary, daily life. You will ignore none of these, yet they will have no more pull on you than your dirty laundry. Freely, easily, you'll let go of everything, and thus obtain everything. As you obtain everything, you will be able to give it all to others. Work hard and make this happen!

### Hold onto Your Center and Let Everything Flow

People tend to make all kinds of judgments based on what they see or hear, but you really shouldn't tie yourself up in fixed views like this. When Sakyamuni Buddha wanted to save an insect, sometimes he became that insect. He had to first become one with that creature's mind, and then it wouldn't resist his help.

---

**14. Karmic affinity**(因緣)**:** The connection or attraction between people or things, due to previous karmic relationships.

내가 예전에 소로길을 가다가 가재가 기어 나오는데, 그걸 구해 주려고 손을 뻗치니까, 가재가 앞발을 딱 들고선 요러고 (양 손바닥을 펴 어깨 위로 들어 보이시며) 대항을 하고 그럽디다. 그걸 보고 "가재를 건질 때는 내가 가재가 돼야 그 가재를 건질 수가 있다." 하는 부처님 말씀이 딱 떠오르는 겁니다.

그런데 모습이 인간일 뿐이지 우리 마음 안에는 헤아릴 수 없는 천차만별의 모습들과 헤아릴 수 없이 많은 중생의 마음이 있는데 그런 것들을 어떻게 제거할 수 있겠습니까?

'내' 속에 있는 자생 중생들의 의식들이 자꾸 마음을 자아내어, 자기한테 해롭게 하기도 하고, 즐겁게 하기도 하고, 때론 화나게 하기도 하면서, 일거수일투족이 다 이러는데, 우리는 거기에 속아서, 자기가 원래 그러는 줄 알고, 그대로 자기가 하는 거라고 느낀다는 겁니다. 그러니, 그렇게 느끼는 대로, 자기는 그렇게 생각되는 대로 행동을 하고 생활하고 가게 되는 거죠. 그러면 그게 고가 되는 거예요.

Years ago, when I was walking through a forest, I came across a crawfish sitting in the middle of the trail. It had ended up quite a ways from the nearby stream, so I bent down, intending to pick it up and carry it back to the water. But as I reached for the crawfish, it held up its claws, waving them at me as if to fight me off. As soon as I saw this, I knew what the Buddha had meant: In order to save a crawfish, you have to become one with it. Even a crawfish!

Although we ourselves now have a human shape, we're filled with consciousnesses of every kind of level. These unenlightened consciousnesses give rise to every kind of feeling and thought. Sometimes they make us happy, at other times they cause us to feel miserable, and at still other times they cause us to feel angry.

But they're deceiving us. Those thoughts are arising from inside us, so we mistake them for "me," thinking they are "my" feelings. We act on them and make choices based on them. And this is how life becomes suffering.

Yet it's said, "There is no suffering." This is because every single thing you do and experience

그런데 "고가 없다" 이럽니다. 이건 모든 게 찰나찰나 화해서 물 흘러가듯 흘러가고, 뜬구름이 모였다 흩어지며 흘러가듯 그러는 거라 그렇습니다. 이렇게 흘러가는 것을 우리는 뭐라도 잡은 것처럼 쥐고서는, 이것이 어떠니 저것이 어떠니 하고 있습니다.

이런 식으로 애를 쓰고 있으니, 고에서 허덕이는 거 아닙니까? 여러분의 한 생각이 능수하고 지혜롭다면 이런 걸 뛰어넘을 수 있습니다.

고정된 게 하나도 없이 그냥 하나하나 다 화해서 가버리는 거라, 모든 게 공한 겁니다. 나라고 하는 것도 몸 안의 모든 중생과 더불어 같이 살고 있으면서 공해서 돌아가고, 바깥에서도 공해서 돌아가고, 나와 더불어 같이 모두가 공해서 돌아가는데, 병 붙을 자리가 어딨으며, 고가 붙을 자리가 어딨으며, 업이 붙을 자리가 어딨으며, 괴로움이 붙을 자리가 어딨으며, 또 즐거움이 붙을 자리가 어디 있겠습니까?

keeps transforming every instant. It's all flowing like water, like clouds gathering and then drifting away. But here we are, insisting things should be like this, or people should be doing that. As if we had control over any of it! As if we could catch the clouds or grab water in our fists!

How could trying to grab hold of such things lead anywhere other than to suffering? If you're wise enough to just let these things flow past, you can avoid so much unnecessary suffering.

There's not a single thing anywhere that's fixed or stationary. All of it is ceaselessly changing and transforming and flowing away. Thus, it's called empty. Even "I" doesn't exist. Within your body, "I" is a collection of cells and lives that are ceaselessly flowing and changing. Outside your body, this "I" is also part of a ceaselessly changing whole. Each aspect is flowing and transforming, with nothing stationary that we can separate out and label. It's all empty.

Thus, there is no stationary place for illness to stick to, nor any place for suffering to stick to. There's no place for karma, no place for sadness, and no place for even joy to remain.

제가 항상 말씀드리는 것이, 배우가 영화를 하다가 영화가 막을 내리면 그뿐이듯, 우리들 인생도 그렇다는 겁니다. 그러니까 다만 오직 자기 중심 심봉처를 의지하고 돌아가라 이겁니다.

프로펠러나 바퀴가 중심을 잡고 돌듯, 인생살이도 가운데 중심, 심봉을 쥐고서 살아야 합니다. 심봉은 끄떡도 안 하고 힘을 배출하기 때문에, 심봉을 쥐고 그 힘을 잘 이용해 사는 겁니다. 그래서 내 중심처, 심봉을 믿고 의지하며, 모든 걸 거기에 맡겨 놓는 데에는 이유가 붙지 않습니다.

잘하고 못하고, 못나고 잘나고, 여자고 남자고, 낮고 높고, 잘살고 못살고 이걸 떠나서, 오직 내 심봉을 딱 쥐어야 그대로 흘러가듯이 돌아갈 수 있습니다. 이 심봉을 의지한다면 바퀴가 이탈되지 않으니까요.

Think about going to see a movie: It plays for a couple of hours, and then it's over and the curtain comes down. And then, before long, the next movie starts. Our lives, too, are like this. So regardless of what kind of role you're playing, go forward holding fast to your own upright center. All you truly need to do is just hold onto this.

Like a wheel rotates around its axle, we have to make our fundamental mind the center of our lives. We have to live with this great *pillar of mind* [15] at our center. No matter what happens, this pillar never wavers. It's capable of sending forth vast, unimaginable energy. So have faith in this center of yours, rely upon it, and entrust everything there. Unconditionally! Unleash this energy and go forward applying it to everything in your life.

Even when things are going well, even when they go badly, even if your role in life seems meaningless, or even if it seems important – regardless of whether you're male or female,

---

**15. Pillar of mind:** Similar to Jujangja (拄杖子), which is a monk's staff, but the term is used figuratively to refer to our fundamental mind.

이 심봉이라는 건 **반야**[5]줄이라고도 할 수 있고, 자기 주처라고도 할 수 있고, 불성이라고도 할 수 있습니다. 여러 가지로 이름이 다양합니다만, 이름이야 어쨌건 그 중심처만 의지하면서 거기에 모든 걸 맡겨 오직 내가 함이 없이 하면서 돌아간다면, 여러분이 한 찰나에 그냥 그대로, 그대로 자유자재하며 여여하게 살 수 있습니다. 여여한 삶의 보람을 갖는 겁니다.

그런데 지금도 아리송하시죠? 이렇게 말씀을 해 드려도 아리송하시죠? 한 가지를 알면 열 가지를 안다고, 여러분 생활이 고정된 게 하나도 없이 그냥 화해서 찰나찰나 돌아가고 있는데, 뭐가 그리 아리송합니까?

---

**5. 반야**(般若): 대승불교에서 온갖 분별과 망상에서 벗어나 만물의 참다운 실상을 깨닫고 불법의 이치를 꿰뚫어 성불에 이르게 되는 지혜를 뜻함.

sophisticated or clumsy, rich or poor, young or old – when you go forward centered around this great pillar of mind, your life will flow like water. A wheel that's centered on its axle won't come off.

This pillar of mind can be called Buddha-nature, "my true abode," or "the saving power of *Prajna*."[16] It can be given all kinds of names, but regardless of the label, if you rely upon that place, if you utterly entrust everything there, to the extent that you are able to work together as one with everything, without any trace of "me," then you will be able to live in every moment naturally, attuned to the flowing of the whole. Just as you are, you can lead a life of great meaning and worth.

Looking around, it seems like some of you are still unclear about what I'm saying. Yet, as the saying goes, once you understand one thing, ten others will become clear. Everything in your daily life is already flowing away, so what's there to be unclear about? It's all changing and transforming every instant.

---

**16. Prajna:** Insight into the true nature of reality, namely the awareness of impermanence, emptiness, and non-self.

그러니 '아, 이렇구나! 모든 게 물 흐르듯 흘러
가는 거구나. 내 인생도 이렇게 살아야겠구나!' 하
고, 잡지 말고 놓고 가세요. 잡으면 고가 됩니다.

부처님이 나를 깨치게 해서 내 차원을 올려주는
게 아닙니다. 부처님이 여러분한테 행복을 갖다주
는 것도 아닙니다. 그리고 빼앗아 가는 것도 없어
요. 내가 지은 업이 많아서 괴로운 거지 남이 내 행
복을 빼앗는 게 아닙니다. 당연히 남이 나한테 행복
을 가져다주는 것도 아니고요.

모든 건 본인이 하는 대로 오고 가고 하는 건데,
모든 게 쉼 없이 날아가 버리니 도무지 내가 했다
안 했다 할 수 없게끔 되는 겁니다. 그저 찰나찰나
내가 하는 대로 변해서 돌아가는 거뿐입니다.

Look at what's happening in your life – it's all teaching you. "Ah, everything is flowing like water. This is how I need to live as well!" Go forward like this without trying to grasp or cling to things. If you try to seize hold of something, it will become a source of suffering.

Not only is there no moment in your life that you could grab hold of something, there's also no moment for anyone else to grab hold of something. Even the Buddha can't awaken you or raise your spiritual level. He can't bring you happiness, nor can he take it away from you. Everything comes or goes according to our own thoughts and actions. It comes and goes according to the decisions we've made.

Everything is flowing by so quickly that there's no moment of time that you could grab and say, "That's what I've done," or "I didn't do that." It's all flowing and changing every instant in response to what you are doing and thinking.

## 매사를 다하는 보배를 믿고

그러니 여러분한테 어려움이 닥쳤다, 병고가 생겼다 그런 것은 단 한 가지 이유입니다. 지금 인간으로까지 셀 수 없는 진화를 거치면서 단지 살고자 가졌던 관습과 욕심과 착이 그대로 남아 있어 나온 결과입니다. "과거는 묻지 마라. 미래도 생각지 마라. 오늘도 공했다. 공했으니까 찰나찰나 가버리는 것에 착을 두지 마라." 이랬는데도, 오늘날에도 여러분은 여전히 착을 가지고 갑니다.

어쩌니저쩌니 말을 할 순 있겠지만, 마음에 욕심을 두고 착을 두고 하시진 마십시오. 함이 없이 얘기하고, 뭐든 함이 없이 하십시오. 뭔가 일을 할 때도, 흘러 흘러 가는 걸 지켜보면서, "아, 전에는 우리가 이렇게 했으니까, 이번엔 우리가 이렇게 이렇게 하는 게 좋지 않겠어?" 하면서, 그냥 여여하게 그대로 해라 이겁니다. 그 생각이 제일 중요합니다.

## This Treasure can Take Care of Everything

You need to know this: Whatever hardship you're facing, whatever illness or suffering you're going through, ultimately those all have only one cause – your own mind. It's the *habits*,[17] desires, and attachments you've created through life after life. Don't try to figure out your past life, and don't worry about your future. Even this very moment is empty. Everything passes by. Everything is going away at every instant. Yet, even though I tell people this, they still try to cling to things.

I'm not saying to never have opinions or speak, just that when you do, you need to let go of your attachments and grasping to whatever it is. Also when you're working on something, pay attention to how things are flowing. Keep entrusting everything like this. Then you'll be able to respond to the situation naturally and harmoniously. "Last year we handled that problem like this. Would that work now?" Being able to respond from your foundation like this is so important.

---

**17. Habits**(習): These include not just the ways of thought and behavior learned in this life, but also all of those tendencies of thought and behavior that have accumulated over endless eons.

모든 것은 여러분이 어떤 생각을 가지고 어떤 마음으로 말을 하고 행동하며 사느냐에 달린 겁니다.

그냥 이 심봉을 붙들고 의지하라고 그랬더니, 거기에 일체를 몰락 놓으라는 뜻인지 모르고, 자기 생각으로 심봉을 붙잡고는 이름만 부르면서 붙들고 있는 거예요. 그거는 고를 만들어 붙드는 거와 같아요.

사실, 의지해서 부르는 그 **주인공**[6]이라는 것도 이름이고 말일 뿐이라 그것조차도 놓고 불러야 되는데 말이에요.

---

**6. 주인공**(主人空): 우리 모두 스스로 갖추어 가지고 있는 근본마음으로 일체 만물만생의 근본과 직결된 자리. 나를 존재하게 하고, 나를 움직이게 하며, 내 모든 것을 관장하는 참 주인이므로 주인(主人)이며, 매 순간 쉴 사이 없이 변하고 돌아가 고정된 실체가 없으므로 비어 있다고 할 수 있기 때문에 빌 공(空)자를 써서, 주인공(主人空)이라 함. 본래면목, 성품, 불성 등 여러 가지로 지칭할 수 있음.

Everything in your life depends upon where your thoughts, words, and actions are coming from.

When I say that you need to cling to this pillar of mind, I mean that you need to entrust everything there, utterly and unconditionally, without looking back. But people often miss this point, and instead just keep repeating the words "pillar of mind" or "*Juingong*."[18] Merely repeating the names like this is just reaching deep into your own suffering and grasping it that much tighter.

In fact, even the foundation, Juingong, that we rely upon is just a name, a word. So we have to entrust everything without holding onto even that.

---

**18. Juingong** (主人空): Pronounced "ju-in-gong." Juin (主人) means the true doer or the master, and gong (空) means empty. Thus Juingong is our true nature, our true essence, the master within that is always changing and manifesting, without a fixed form or shape.

Daehaeng Sunim has compared Juingong to the root of the tree. Our bodies and consciousness are like the branches and leaves, but it is the root that is the source of the tree, and it is the invisible root beneath the ground that sustains the visible tree.

"심봉을 의지하고 돌아가라. 여여하게 돌아가라." 그랬더니 '심봉, 주인공(主人空)' 이런 이름만 부르면서 그걸 붙들고 있어요.

내 근본, 내 주인공을 믿고 의지하는 마음이 지극하면, 일거수일투족 거기다 의지하는 마음이 지극하면, 감사함도 거기 있고, 즐거움도 거기 있고, 슬플 때 같이 붙들고 울 수도 있는 위안도 거기에 있음을 알 것입니다. 심봉인 근본자리는 매사를 다 할 수 있는 보배입니다, 보배!

## 뛰어넘는 한생각의 소중함

그렇게 심중을 굳히고 '의지할 수 있는 데는 여기밖에 없다.' 하고 모든 걸 그냥 거기에 맡기면 알아서 일이 흘러가게 돼 있는데, 그렇게 하기보다는 개인적으로 뭔가를 원하는 마음이 크다 보니 욕심, 탐심, 치심으로 이리저리 재면서 모든 거에 간섭하는 거예요. 저기 뭐, 똥 굴러가는 것만 봐도, 저 똥이 어디로 굴러가느냐고 야단입니다. 허허허, 참내!

Although I keep saying, "You need to entrust this pillar of mind with everything and then just let all things in your daily life flow in tune with it," there are still some people who are just repeating the words "Juingong" and "pillar of mind." As if that would do any good.

If you keep working on utterly relying upon and trusting your own pillar of mind, your Juingong, and are entrusting it with every thought, every worry, every problem that arises, you will find gratitude and joy in the middle of all that. And when you are sad, you will find solace and a shoulder to cry upon. This fundamental mind of yours is a treasure that can take care of everything. It's such a treasure!

### A Single Thought is So Precious!

So make a very firm decision that "This fundamental mind is the only thing I'm going to rely upon!" If you entrust everything with this attitude, it will all naturally flow towards the best outcome. However, if your desire for something is greater than your willingness to let go, you'll end up

아, 새들도요, 저 마당에 먹을 거를 뿌려 주면요, 사람이 드나들지 않는 데 있는 걸 먹어요. 새들이 진짜 모이를 먹기 원하면, 그냥 다 주고 물러나세요. 그러면 알아서 먹습니다.

자기 근본에 모든 걸 믿고 맡기는 것에 신경을 써야 하는데, 그렇게는 안 하고, 남의 일 참견 다 하고 또 남의 탓은 다 하고 그럽니다. 지금 빌딩에 불이 나서 자기 살 구멍을 찾아 나가야 하는 그 순간에 남의 탓을 할 사이가 있습니까?

게다가 자식과 부모는 그 무엇보다도 이미 강하게 연결되어 있어서, 무조건 그 심봉에 다 맡겨 놓고 하나로 돌아가게 하라고 그렇게 일러주는데도, 입으로 망해 버려요! '주인공'이라고 하는 건 말뿐이고, 애들한테 막말을 하면서 소리를 지르지요.

assessing things through the eyes of covetousness, foolishness, and desperation. And then you'll start meddling and getting involved in all kinds of things. Do you know how much noise some people make when they see dried dog poop on the sidewalk? It's just old dog poop! [Laughs.]

When I scatter birdseed in the yard, the birds all go to the seed that's farthest away from people. They go where there's no people moving around. If you want them to enjoy that birdseed, you have to step back and leave them alone.

People need to work at relying upon their foundation, but instead they spend their time blaming others or complaining about what they're doing, or even meddling in their lives. Do you really have time for that? The house is on fire! You have only a few moments to find a way out! Are you really going to spend this time standing around criticizing others?

In the case of parents and children, there's already a close connection there, so if you just rely upon your pillar of mind and trust it, things between you will work out quite well. But careless words will make a mess of your relationship.

"요놈의 새끼야, 응? 배울 시기에 배워야지, 하라는 공부는 안 하고 어떻게 이럴 수가 있어?"라고 하면서 펄펄 뛰고 온통 난리가 납니다.

그러면 애들이 따뜻함을 못 느껴서 달아나가요. 공부도 그렇고, 여러 가지 힘들다는 얘기를 하면, 그게 뭐가 그렇게 힘드냐고 윽박지릅니다. 그럼, 애들이 그냥 다 내던지고 달아나가요.

그러니까 이 마음 하나만 의지하고, 모든 것을 놓고 가야 됩니다. "모든 것을 놓고 가야 한다."가 아니라, 본래 모든 것을 놓고 가는 거니까, 그냥 어느 것에도 착을 두지 말라 이겁니다. 뛰어넘는 **한생각**[7]이 있어야 내 가정도, 살림살이도 달라지게 돼요. 어떻게들 생각하십니까?

---

**7. 한생각**: 어떤 생각을 우리 내면의 근본자리에 입력시키거나 맡겨 놓았을 때, 근본을 통해 나오는 생각은 우리 몸속의 모든 생명들뿐만 아니라 이 세상의 만물만생에 전달되며, 일체가 그 생각에 응하게 됨. 보이지 않는 정신계, 즉 우리 근본마음을 통해 일으켜지는 생각은 물질계에서 현실로 나타나게 됨. 이렇게 근본을 통해 나오게 되는 생각을 한생각이라 함.

Instead of trying to actually get in touch with their own fundamental mind, some people shout at their children, saying things like, "What the hell are you doing? Why aren't you doing your homework? Do you think you're so smart that you don't even need to study for exams?"

If your home is filled with arguing and shouting over every little thing, if, when your children complain about how hard school is or about problems with other kids, they hear in return, "You don't know what hard is! My life is hard! Do you know how hard I work to…," they won't thrive. If they don't feel any warmth at home, if it isn't a comfortable place, they'll stay away as much as possible, or even run away.

So you must let go of everything and just rely upon this one pillar of mind. In truth, everything is already flowing, so just try to not cling to ideas or events. If, with a wise thought, you can leap over these things, your life and family will be relaxed and comfortable. Wouldn't this be a better way to live?

이 말이 오늘 법문 중에 가장 귀중한 말입니다. 우리 인생도 찰나찰나 프로펠러 돌아가듯 돌아가기 때문에 거기에 병이든 뭐든 붙을 게 없어요.

그런 믿음 하나 챙겨서 모든 걸 놓고 가라는데도 그러질 못합니다. 세상이 어떻게 돌아가는지 그 상황을 있는 그대로 얘기해 주는데도, 그걸 진짜로 믿질 못하고 왜곡되게 사시니까 힘든 겁니다.

진리대로 살면 얼굴도 허옇게 피고 아마도 사는 날까진 잘 살다 갈 수 있을 겁니다.

### 마음공부의 영원한 공덕

그리고 이 **마음공부**[8]한 건 어디 안 가요. 영원히 여러분과 같이 가는 겁니다. 왜냐? 여러분이 계속 진화되는 데 쓰이는 거니까요.

---

**8. 마음공부**: 진정한 자유인이 되기 위해 자신의 마음이 어떻게 작용하고 변하는지를 관찰하고 배우며, 그것을 실제 생활 속에서 응용하고 체험해 보면서 알아가는 모든 과정을 뜻함.

What I've just said is the most important thing I'll say all day. It's so precious! Our lives continuously flow and change, as fast and ceaselessly as a spinning propeller. In the midst of all this flowing, there's no place for anything to stick to.

Even though I tell people that there's inherently no place for illness to stick to, they don't seem to believe it. I'm just telling you about how the world works, nothing more, and yet people still don't make an effort to live in accordance with this. Instead, they follow distorted paths, living upside-down lives, and end up experiencing every kind of hardship.

If they could just live in tune with this truth that everything is already flowing and moving through their fundamental mind, they would radiate joy and wisdom, and would live out their full, proper span of years.

### Learn the Ways of a Free Person

Let me be clear, what you attain through this practice won't fade away. It will be with you forever. Why? Because it's something you'll use continuously as you evolve.

궁극적으로는 자기가 어떤 모습을 갖고, 어떤 차원으로 살 건지 자유권을 갖게 됩니다. 이 지구 안이 아닌 다른 상세계에 태어나든 별성이 되든 뭐가되든, 하여튼 자기 자신이 자발적으로 선택해서 나올 수 있어요.

누구나 자유롭게 될 수 있다고 했습니다. 그런데 자유는 누구에게나 있다 하더라도 그렇게 할 수있는 방법을 알아야 자유롭게 할 수 있는 거 아닙니까! 집 하나를 세우려 해도 주춧돌도 있어야 하고, 기둥도 있어야 하고, 대들보도 있어야 하고 서까래도 있어야 하고, 지붕도 올려놔야 하고, 그렇게 알아야 할 것도 많고 해야 할 일도 많은데, 하물며 차원을 넘나드는 상태가 되려면, 차근차근 배우고 알아가야 되겠죠.

Ultimately, if you keep working at this, you will be free. Free to choose your shape and appearance, free to choose the level you'll be reborn at, free to be born on this planet or to choose another planet, or even a star, or somewhere else entirely. Anyway, you'll be able to choose whatever kind of life you'll have going forward.

Even though everyone is inherently free, you have to learn how to behave freely in order to actually become free. You need to learn to take what you understand, put it into practice, and keep doing this. Start with where you are. Look at how we build a house. You start by leveling the dirt and building a solid foundation. Then you need to build the walls, floor, and roof. You have to figure out how to do all of this to end up with a useful building.

Even to build just a house, there are so many things you have to know and be able to do. How much more is there, then, if you want to know what it truly means to be free? So you'd better get started learning these things one by one, and stage by stage.

그래서 옛날에 부처님께서 "내 가죽을 얻었느냐? 내 살을 얻었느냐? 내 뼈를 얻었느냐? 내 정수를 얻었느냐?" 이런 질문들을 던지신 겁니다. 선지식들도 이런 문제를 가지고 말씀하셨고요.

하지만 배우는 우리는 상근기, 중근기, 하근기 이런 걸 따질 게 아니라, 배운 걸 실천하고, 그리고 그걸 뛰어넘고, 이 과정을 반복해 가다 보면 상근기나, 중근기, 하근기를 따지지 않아도 그런 게 뭔지 보면 알고, 들으면 알고, 그냥 다 알게 돼 있어요.

많은 사람이 가정에 복잡한 문제가 생기면, 어떻게 하냐고 나한테 물으러 오시는데, 때로는 이렇게 이렇게 하시라고 일러 드립니다. 그래서 그 한 가지는 어떻게 잘 넘어갔다고 칩시다. 근데 그다음에 오는 건 어떻게 할 겁니까? 그럴 때마다 사사건건 남한테 도와 달라고 할 겁니까? 언제까지 그럴 건데요?

This is why the Buddha tested his disciples, asking, "Have you grasped my skin?" "Have you grasped my flesh?" "Have you grasped my bones?" and, "Have you grasped my essence?" *Seon*[19] masters have said similar things to their students.

That said, you shouldn't concern yourself with other people's level of spiritual practice, or compare yourself to them. Just focus on putting into practice what you've learned, and then move on from that. If you keep doing this over and over, you'll naturally begin to understand everything about different levels of spiritual awareness.

Sometimes when people come to see me with some desperate problem, I'll tell them very specifically what to do, and that will usually take care of it. So, they've gotten past one particularly ugly problem, but when the next thing arises, what will happen to them? Will their only hope be to go find someone else to take care of it for them? Will this

---

**19. Seon** (禪) (Chan, Zen): Seon describes the unshakeable state where one has firm faith in their inherent foundation, their Buddha-nature, and so returns everything they encounter back to this fundamental mind. It also means letting go of "I," "me," and "mine" throughout one's daily life.

그래서 마음공부를 하라는 겁니다. 그런데 원래 마음공부라는 게 하다 보면, 뭔가 딱히 '안다'라고 할 게 없다는 걸 느끼게 됩니다. 그냥 세상 돌아가는 이치고 진리라서 그래요. 하지만 그걸 진실하게 실천하고 살다 보면, 어떤 게 와도 대처할 수 있게 됩니다. 일체가 근본을 통해 둘이 아니게 돌아가는 이 도리를 알게 되면, 어떠한 게 와도, 아니 귀신이 떼거리로 몰려온대도 "허허" 하고 웃을 겁니다. 왜냐하면 모든 게 둘이 아닌 까닭이라 그렇습니다.

그런데 정신 상태가 온전치 못한 사람은, 스스로 어떻게 해 볼 수가 없기 때문에 가족들은 더 많이 노력해서 근본마음이 서로 연결되도록 최선을 다해야 합니다. 저는 가족들의 이러한 정성 들이는 것과는 별개로, 무조건 내 마음을 그쪽으로 주든지, 아니면 그쪽의 마음을 내 쪽으로 가져오든지 해서 고칩니다.

be their life every time something ugly arises? If that's the case, it won't turn out well.

This is why I keep urging you to work at relying upon your fundamental mind and to learn how it works. That said, the deeper your practice goes, the more you'll realize there is no "I know" or "I gained," because you'll understand that everything is constantly flowing as one, and that not a single thing has been added. You have to truly and sincerely put this into practice, and then you can take care of whatever arises. If you can see whatever confronts you as part of yourself, as something that's not separate, then even if all the ghosts in the world were to swarm at you, you'd just smile and chuckle.

Why? Because you're one with them. The fingers on one hand never hurt each other, do they? It's the same reality.

When it comes to people suffering from severe mental illness, well, they often can't practice for themselves, so the family has to work that much harder at practicing so that they can connect with them through their fundamental mind. In this way, family can bring the energy of our fundamental

자기 근본마음을 항상 철저히 믿고 이 공부를 하는 사람들은 이런 일로 고통받는 사람들의 등불이 되어줄 수 있습니다. 그런 일은 약을 먹인다든가 상담한다고 해서 완전히 해결되는 게 아닙니다. 증상을 완화시킬 순 있어도 근본적으로 낫게 하는 게 아니며 의사가 할 수 있는 일들에는 한계가 있습니다. 그저 이 근본마음을 통하는 거 외에는 완전히 해결할 수 있는 방법이 없어요. 그런 건 영계성, 업보성, 유전성, 세균성, 인과성으로 온 것들이 의식들 속에 다 끼여서 일어난 거라 그래요.

mind to bear on the situation. Of course, I also do what I can to help by giving them some of the energy of my mind, or, if they've lived a gentle, generous life, I can put their mind into mine.

If someone persistently works at having faith in their inherent Buddha-nature, and is trying to trust it with whatever comes up, they too can be a light to those who suffer.

In cases of mental illnesses like this, no amount of pills or therapy will completely cure the illness. There are some things that doctors can help with, but they can't solve problems caused by the consciousnesses of the lives within us. These consciousnesses were created and conditioned through karma, genetics, ghosts, microbes, and the conditioned nature of existence, and so the only real way to dissolve them is through our fundamental mind.

Thus, the best way to help people in this situation is to help them through mind so that they can eventually take all of these karmic consciousnesses and return them to their own fundamental mind.

그러니 모든 게 공했다는 거를 알고 마음을 편안하게 두어 그냥 휙휙 넘어가게끔 하세요. 그냥 내 근본마음에 의지해 그 기둥 하나만 딱 붙들고 있으면, 아무리 모진 바람이 불어도 날아가진 않아요. 폐일언하고, 그냥 모든 걸 다 내 근본마음에 끌어다 놓아야 합니다. 그렇게 함으로써 그런 병에 시달리는 가족도 환자도 이겨낼 수 있습니다.

마음에서 고장 난 거, 의식에서 고장 난 거는 마음을 통해 마음으로 고쳐야 합니다. 그런데 사실, 천차만별이 다 마음에서 일어난 일입니다. 내가 형성된 것도, 이 차원의 이 모습을 가지고 지금 내가 사는 것도 다 내 마음에 의한 것입니다. 영화나 드라마에 나오는 배우처럼 배역을 하나 맡아 그 소임을 하고 있는 거지요. 단지 이 소임은 남이 준 게 아니라, 내가 만들어서 가지고 나온, 내가 나한테 준 소임입니다.

Remind them that everything is working together as one in this flowing whole, and encourage them to put their mind at ease and quickly move through the things that confront them, entrusting them one by one, and then moving on.

If you, too, go forward like this, focused on only your fundamental mind, this great pillar, then no matter how bitter a wind should blow, you won't be swept off your feet. In a word, take it all and introduce it to your fundamental mind. In this way, you'll be able to help the patients as well as their families get through the illness.

If the mind has problems, then it's through this fundamental mind that those must be solved. In fact, every last thing in the world is something that's been created through mind. Your mind is what caused you to be born into this world, it created the life you lead now, so it's what can take care of all this and help you fulfill the role you were born to play. Understand that no one else assigned you this role. You made it and assigned it to yourself.

그러니까 지금 사는 게 한 철 소임임을 알고, 이런 것도 저런 것도 붙들 게 없음을 아십시오. 붙들지 않으면 업도 붙을 게 없고, 고도 붙을 게 없고, 병도 붙을 게 없습니다.

이런 건전한 생각으로, '주인공' 그 줄만 잡고서, 모든 것을 거기다가 맡기고, 감사하게 생각하고 가세요. 어떠한 일이 닥치든 내 주인공, 근본마음을 믿고, 모든 걸 거기다 맡겨 상황을 바꾸는, 찰나찰나 대처할 수 있는, 그런 능력을 기르십시오.

그러면 그것으로써 인생살이는 족하게 할 수 있습니다.

### 전깃줄이 맞붙어야 불이 들어온다

이렇게 내가 자꾸 얘기해도, 여러분들은 당연히 잘 모르십니다. 하지만 내가 자기 근본을 진짜로 믿고 거기에 모든 걸 맡기면서 생활하라는 거는, 자기

But please understand that even this role is just a temporary thing. None of it is anything to get attached to. If you aren't reaching out and trying to grab onto karma, then karma, too, has no way to stick to you. Hardships won't find a place to grab hold, and illnesses, likewise, won't be able to find a foothold.

Keep this wonderful fact in mind and stay focused on Juingong. Stay focused on your foundation like it was a lifeline, and entrust everything there with gratitude. Develop your ability to cope with whatever comes to you by taking everything, in each moment, and entrusting it to your fundamental mind.

Then, whatever adversity you face will change. If you go forward with nothing more in life than this ability, it will still be enough for you to live without undue want or hardship.

### Stop Digging the Hole, and Instead Trust Your Inherent Light

It's completely understandable if you don't yet grasp what I'm saying. But the reason I keep

가 그걸 알든 모르든 상관없이 그렇게 해야만 일에 대처하는 능력도 생기고 인생을 여여하게 살아갈 수 있기 때문입니다. 그렇게 하면, 그냥 그대로 한 소식 넘어간 겁니다.

그런데 '아이고, 내가 배우지도 못하고, 잘 알지도 못하니, 내가 어떻게 그분같이 그렇게 할 수 있을까?' 이렇게 생각한단 말입니다. 그 생각이 탈인 거예요. 그러니 집안에서건 밖에서건 그냥 넘어갈 일도, 생각으로 붙들어서 오히려 일을 벌이고 망가뜨리지 마세요.

그리고 일이 벌어지면, 이거 어떡하느냐고 또 뛰어옵니다. 내가 볼 때 어떻겠습니까? '세상에! 그냥 갈 수 있는 일을 왜 이렇게 만들어서, 분란을 일으켜 가지곤 또 왔나? 허허 참, 기가 막혀서!' 이렇게 혼잣말로 이럽니다.

saying that you need to trust your foundation and entrust everything to it is because that is the only way you can develop the deep ability to truly solve whatever you face. This is the only way to truly live peacefully and at ease, regardless of what arises in your life. If you can do this, you've taken one giant step forward on the path.

But instead, people get caught up in thoughts like "How could I practice like *Kun Sunim*[20] does? I don't know what I'm doing! I'm not at the same level she is." It's these thoughts that are the problem. People take situations and problems that they should have been able to pass through fairly quickly and turn them into quagmires. They create all kinds of unnecessary work and hardship.

Then, after they've made things worse, they come to me, asking for help. It's so frustrating. I wish I could say how I really feel when they bring me these things! "Oh, for crying out loud! Why did you make such a mess out of something that

------

20. **Sunim / Kun Sunim:** Sunim is the respectful title of address for a Buddhist monk or nun in Korea, and Kun Sunim is the title given to outstanding nuns or monks.

이런 답답한 걸 어디에다가 말을 합니까! 그럴 때마다 난 이렇게 말해 주죠. "그저 열심히 **관**[9]하세요. 진실하게 관하면 나도 거기 도와주게 돼 있어요. 그러니 진정코 진실하게 관하세요."라고요.

그러면 얼마 안 있어서 와 가지곤 "아이고, 스님! 해결했습니다. 참 고맙습니다." 글쎄, 이래요. 그러면 그 답답함에 때로는 화가 나서, "당신도 전깃줄이 있고, 나도 전깃줄이 있어요. 근데 그게 맞붙었기 때문에 불이 들어왔을 뿐인데, 고맙긴 뭐가 고맙습니까? 고맙게 생각하려거든 당신 주인공한테나 고맙게 생각하세요!" 이러고 맙니다. 아이, 이거 정말이지, 나는 이걸 사람들한테 가르치는 게 이렇게 힘드는 줄 몰랐습니다.

---

**9. 관(觀)**: 어의적으로 '관찰하다' '보다' 라는 뜻을 가지고 있으며, 마음공부를 하는 과정에서는 '참나'인 주인공을 믿고 맡기는 것을 뜻함. 즉, 삶에서 부딪치는 모든 문제들을 주인공만이 해결할 수 있다는 철저한 믿음으로 주인공에게 맡겨 놓고 집착 없이 지켜보는 것을 통틀어 '관'이라 함.

wouldn't have caused any problems? Why do you keep blowing things up, and then asking me for help with them?"

But I can't say these things out loud! Instead, I just look for what people need to move forward and go from there. "Okay. Focus on entrusting it all and observing. If you're sincerely letting go, then my mind will be there as well, and will help you. So deeply, truly, trust your root and turn everything over to it. Then, just go forward while being aware."

Before long, they come back, saying, "It worked! Thank you so much!" But frankly, sometimes this leaves me feeling frustrated and irritated, because they keep making an unnecessary mess out of things time after time, so that it doesn't seem like they've learned anything at all.

So sometimes I'll respond with, "'Thanks?' Thanks for what? It turned out well because you worked at trusting your own fundamental mind. You have your own fundamental mind, as do I. These are like electrical wires, and when they connect, the energy flows back and forth, and the light comes on. If you want to thank something,

하지만 나는 내 몸뚱이가 가루가 된다고 하더라도 이 한 가지, 진리를 여러분에게 알려 주고자 합니다. 내 근본마음을 진실로 믿고 거기에 일체를 맡겨 놓고 가야만, 이 공기주머니를 벗어나 자유자재해질 수 있습니다.

그게 자신을 구하는 길이고 세계를 구하는 길입니다. 여러분이 이 도리를 진실로 깨닫기 만을 바라는 이 마음이야말로 내가 가지고 있는 모두입니다. 세상을 다 줄 테니 그만두라는 유혹을 한다고 하더라도 그렇게 할 수가 없습니다.

여러분들이 시주한답시고 돈을 하늘만큼 땅만큼 가져온대도 소용이 없습니다. 여러분들이 진정으로 자기 근본마음을 믿지 못한다면 공덕이 안 됩니다.

then feel grateful to this fundamental mind, this Juingong of yours that made that possible." I truly didn't appreciate just how hard it is to get people to have faith in this treasure they're carrying around within themselves.

Even if it takes every last drop of my blood, I want to make everyone grasp just one thing: Deeply trust this foundation of yours, and entrust every single thing there. Let go and entrust it. Only then will you be free in the truest sense, and able to move beyond the limitations of the human realm.

This is the way you can save yourself, and the way you can save the world. I want nothing more than for you all to awaken to this truth. This is the focus of all my efforts. Even if someone were to offer me all the kingdoms of the Earth, I wouldn't turn away from this.

Even if someone brings a van full of cash and asks me to solve some problem they're facing, it's pointless if they don't have faith in their foundation. If they don't trust their own foundation, there's no energy going back and forth, and so no benefit can come from their offering.

여러분들이 돈 가져오는 거로 밥 먹고 살 양으로 내가 중노릇하는 거 아닙니다. 그렇게 한다면 죽어야죠. 아니, 죽는 문제는 차치하고 벌써 저 땅속에 사는 저 하천세계 벌레로 떨어질 겁니다.

그런데요, 난 여러분을 위해서라면 하천세계로 떨어진들 겁나는 거 없습니다. 생각이 다 있으니까요.

질문하실 분 있다고요? 그런데 말입니다, 질문 받기 전에 한마디 더 할게요. 우리가 걸음을 걸을 때, 이미 떼어 놓은 뒷발짝을 잡고 가는 게 아닌 것처럼, 생활할 때도 그렇게 자연스럽게 놓고 가시라 했습니다. 그러면 모든 게 고정된 게 없이 돌아가게 되니까 병 붙을 것도 없고, 업 붙을 것도 없고, 고 붙을 것도 없습니다.

I didn't become a sunim for the sake of living off your offerings. If I did, I'd deserve death. Actually, setting aside the issue of dying, living like that would lower the level of my existence so much that in my next life I would naturally be drawn towards the body of a burrowing insect.

But if it's necessary to help you, I'm not afraid of being born with even such a shape. But don't need to worry, I know how to get out of there! [Sunim and the audience laugh.]

It looks like there are people who want to ask questions today, so let me say just one more thing: When we walk, we just go forward naturally, don't we? Is there anyone who tries to pick up and keep their footprints? No. So in the rest of your daily life as well, go forward freely, letting go of everything. Then, because everything is inherently flowing and changing without cease, there will be no place for illness to stick to, no place for karma to land, and no place for hardships to grab hold of you.

Because everything is flowing like this, the thoughts you give rise to have a huge influence. They can cause your family to thrive, or to fall into a dark place from which they may never arise. It's

그리고 그런 가운데서 자기 마음을 어떻게 내느냐에 따라 가정이 흥해질 수도 있고, 아주 한데 떨어져서 일으켜 세울 수도 없는 상태가 되기도 하는 겁니다. 그런데 이렇게 얘기해 줘도 그게 안 되다 보니, 살 집도 없어지게 되고, 아주 파탄이 나는 상황이 벌어지게 되는 거예요.

그럴 땐, 극단적으로 임시방편이라도 일러 주지 않을 수가 없어요. 왜냐하면 너무 고통스러워하니깐요. 스스로 어떻게 해 볼 수는 없으니까요. 그럴 땐 "아주 진실하게 관하면, 귀인이 생기게 돼요. 그러니까 열심히 관하세요."라고 말해 줍니다. 그럭하고, 그 귀인은 근본마음을 통해 부처님께서 나투어 주시게끔 합니다. 제가 이렇게라도 말하면서 해 나가는 이 심정을 여러분은 잘 아셔야 될 겁니다.

여러분이 눈물을 세 동이를 흘린다면, 나는 아마 다섯, 여섯 동이를 흘릴 겁니다, 뼈아프게 말입니다. 여러분을 살리려다 보면 어떨 땐, 제가 구더기나 진드기가 돼야 할 상황도 벌어지지만 그렇게 된다고 하더라도 겁날 일은 없습니다. 진드기로 그냥 그렇게 고정되어 있는 게 아니기 때문이죠.

unfortunate that even though I tell people about this in such detail, so many of them still don't seem to be able to put it into practice. They go and put themselves in desperate situations, where they face losing everything, even their home.

Then, because the situation is so desperate, and they're suffering so much, I have no choice but to give them something miraculous to hang onto. I have no choice because the situation is so bad and they don't yet have the skills to get themselves out of it. So I may tell them that if they work sincerely and truly at entrusting their situation, then someone special will appear and help them. I hope you understand how much I hate having to say things like this in order to get people to start trusting their foundation. Anyway, then, through this inner Buddha, I arrange for help to find them.

Listen, when you hurt, I hurt too. When you cry a bucket full of tears, I shed two or three. It's that painful. When I help people, sometimes I have to become a maggot or a tick. But I'm not afraid of that because I know that even those forms aren't fixed and unchanging.

Please think carefully about the implications of this, and don't be afraid of letting go and trusting

그 뜻을 잘 아셔서 겁내지 마세요. 죽는다고 해도 겁내지 말고, 하늘이 무너진다 해도 겁내지 말고, 내 살림이 이 시점에서 그냥 거덜이 난다 해도 겁내지 마세요. 자기 심봉에 의지해 겁내지 않고 당당하게 가면, 비록 내 눈엔 보이지 않지만, 그 보이지 않는 힘들이 주변에서 다 보고 있다가, "너는 이렇게 하고 너는 저렇게 해라." 하면서 도와줍니다.

뭐, 우리가 그런 거에 **독성(獨聖)**[10]이나 신장(神將), 관세음보살 등등 이름도 많이 지어 놓지 않았습니까? 저 TV에 나오는 애들 만화영화 있죠? '배추 도사, 무 도사' 말이에요. 그것처럼 몸을 바꾸어 변신해 가면서 사람들을 돌봐 줍니다. 그런 게 보살행이에요.

---

**10. 독성(獨聖):** 우리나라 불교 고유의 신앙 대상인 나반존자(那畔尊者)의 다른 이름. 나반존자는 부처님의 뜻에 의해 열반에 들지 않고 말세의 중생을 위해 홀로 천태산에 머물면서 그들에게 복을 준다고 알려져 있음.

your foundation, no matter what arises. Don't let anything intimidate you! Even if you are about to die, don't be afraid. Even if the world is about to explode, don't be afraid. Even if your job and savings disappear, don't be afraid. If you rely upon your own centered mind, standing up straight and without fear, then the unseen energy all around you will take notice and respond to your centered mind, helping you find a way forward.

There are all kinds of stories about this kind of help. Stories about the Bodhisattva of Compassion, or the Hermit Sage, or Dharma-Protecting Warriors. Here in Korea, we even have them in children's cartoons. You've all seen the one with Master Cabbage and Master White Radish,[21] haven't you? They transform their bodies into any form or being that's needed, and then go help people. This is the functioning of a *bodhisattva*.[22]

---

**21.** These were two superhero-type characters from the Korean cartoon series, "Once Upon a Time" (옛날 옛적에).

**22. Bodhisattva:** This usually refers to a person of great spiritual ability who is dedicated to saving those lost in ignorance and suffering. But it also means the applied energy of our fundamental nature, used to help save beings. It can also be described as the non-dual wisdom of enlightenment being used to help others awaken for themselves.

그러니 겁낼 게 뭐 있겠어요? 내가 보살을 항상 모시고 있는데 말이에요. 자기 속에 부처, 보살, 법신 다 모시고 있는데 뭐가 겁납니까? 하여튼 만 분을 모신다고 하더라도 넘쳐서 두드러지지도 않고, 만 분을 다 쓴다 해도 줄지 않으니까, 그 법이 아주 영묘한 거죠. 이렇게 말씀드려도 납득이 안 가신다면, 도대체 어떤 말로 더 설명해 드려야 될까요? 허허허.

(질문자에게) 이제 질문해 보세요.

## 재산이 많아도 분수에 맞고 검소하게

**질문자 1(남)** 일반적으로 배부르고 등 따시면, 마음공부 하기가 참 힘들다는 생각이 듭니다. 내가 여유로우면 주위 사람들을 잘 돌보고 도와줄 것 같은데, 그게 잘 안됩니다.

일단 내 삶이 편안하다 보니까 안일해서 그런지, 옆 사람을 안 돌아보게 돼요. 자비심도 별로 일지 않고요. 나중엔 바뀔 수도 있겠지만, 지금은 그렇습니다. 그래서 역경이 닥치게 되고 역경이 닥치면 그

So there's no reason to be scared. You all have this kind of a bodhisattva within you. Right there, within you, are Buddhas, bodhisattvas, and Dharma protectors. So what's there to be scared of? There's no limit to the number of helpers you have within you. Even if you have a million of them within you, they fit perfectly, without any crowding. And even if you use a million of them, they never decrease. Now, if you still don't understand, I'm not sure what else I can say! [Laughs.]

## Be Humble
## Even When You Have Money and Power

**Questioner 1 (Male)**   I've noticed that during those times when my life is going well, I don't think much about spiritual practice. When times were hard, I'd often thought about the things I could do for others if I had some real money, but then when I had money, I mostly used it for myself.

It seems that if my life is comfortable, I forget about spiritual practice. It feels like I also lose my compassion for others. It seems as if people don't

때 그 어려움에서 벗어나려고 공부하게 되지 않나 이런 생각이 듭니다. 스님의 말씀 부탁드립니다.

**큰스님**  제가 전에 어려운 경계가 없으면 공부하기가 어렵다고 그랬죠? 하지만 사실은 그것도 마음먹기에 달렸어요. 어렵지 않은 처지에서는 어렵지 않게 공부할 수 있는 건데, 왜 일을 어렵게 만든 다음에 공부를 합니까?

재산이 많은 게, 그게 자기 건 줄 아세요? 자기 게 아니에요. 그러니 자기 분수를 알고 겸손한 마음으로 검소하게 살아야 합니다. 살면서 겪게 되는 많은 일을 인간이라는 분수에 맞게, 한국이라는 나라가 처한 상황도 잊지 말고, 내 부모가 자손들을 위해 어떻게 지내왔는지도 알아서, 내가 내 분수를 알고 검소해야 합니다.

take an interest in spiritual practice until they're faced with adversity and desperate circumstances. Could you please speak about this?

**Kun Sunim** I've said something similar before, that it often takes adversity to get people working at spiritual practice. While this is true in general, it doesn't have to be this way. What it truly depends upon is how you make up your mind. If you're in a good situation, you can still practice without a lot of hardship or suffering. There's no need to create a bunch of pain in order to practice.

That said, you realize that money and property aren't yours, right? Understand that those things are only something you're managing on behalf of the whole, and live humbly and frugally. Understand that you're going through all of this because you are still only functioning at the human level of development. You're still only at the human level, so be humble in how you respond to the things you face. Don't forget to care for the land that has raised you. Don't forget how much your grandparents and parents suffered for the sake of their children.

익은 벼가 더 고개를 수그리고 허리를 굽힌다는 말이 있죠. 자기가 지금 돈이 많다고 마구 사는 사람들이 있기도 하겠지만, 이 마음공부 하는 사람들은 돈이 있으나 없으나 사는 게 다름이 없이, 매한가지로 살아야 합니다.

절 짓는 데 보태는 것만 불사가 아닙니다. 좀 어려운 집이 있으면 도와주는 것도 불사예요. 부모가 아파서 자식들이 굶고, 애쓰며 사는 소년 · 소녀 가장들도 있고, 돌보는 자식들이 없어 하루하루 힘들게 사는 노인네들도 많습니다. 운 좋게 TV 방송에

Knowing all this, live humbly, as the manager of what comes your way. There's a lot of wisdom in the old expressions "The ripest grain bows low" and "The branches with the most fruit hang the lowest." While there are people who live extravagantly and recklessly, those working at spiritual practice should try to live modestly, whether they have money or not.

Donating money to help build a temple isn't the only way to support Buddhism. Helping people in need is also contributing to Buddhism.[23] There are families where the parents are sick, and the children miss meals. There are elderly people with no children to look after them, and orphaned adolescents who are trying to care for their younger brothers and sisters. Some of these people are lucky enough to come to the attention of TV news programs, and so receive a fair amount of help, but there are many, many more no one ever hears

---

**23.** In Korean, the term used here, bul-sa (佛事), has taken on a meaning of supporting the construction of temple buildings. Being quite expensive, these require a lot of support and time to finish. But here, Daehaeng Sunim is reminding people of the term's original meaning, which is closer to "the work of a Buddha."

라도 나오면 도움을 많이 받겠지만, 그런 자기 사연 알려지는 거 부끄러워하고, 양심이나 자존심이 너무 강한 사람들은 그냥 온전히 애쓰면서 힘들게 살거든요. 겉으로 드러나진 않았지만, 그렇게 고생하며 사는 사람들이 허두룩해요.

그런 부분들을 좀 봐서 함이 없이 도와줘라 이겁니다. 돈이 없으면 모르겠지만, 있으면 좀 도와주고, 없으면 없는 대로 마음으로 도와주세요.

써도 써도 줄지 않는 그 마음 뒀다가 뭐합니까, 네? 마음 한 접시씩 담아서 그냥 크게 펼치세요. 아끼지 마시고요. 마음 아끼느라 미운 사람, 고운 사람 가리면서 주고 안 주고 하지 마십시오. 그런 마음을 가진 사람은 통달을 못 합니다.

### 나와 남을 가르지 않는 마음

**질문자 2(남)** 한 말씀 올리겠습니다. 저는 우리들이 이 세상에 나올 때, 각자가 백지를 하나씩 가지고 나왔다고 생각을 합니다. 그 백지는 무한정으

about. Some people are too ashamed to tell their story to others, and some have so much pride they insist on doing everything by themselves, but all struggle each day just to live. There are so many people living like this, hidden from sight.

So, what I'm saying is that there is no shortage of people in need of your help. Just be sure to do it as spiritual practice, while letting go of any thoughts of "I did." Even if you have no money at all, there is still that portion of helping that you can do through mind.

No matter how much you use this fundamental mind of yours, its energy never decreases. Would you just put it away in a closet and never use it? Give everyone who comes a full helping! Don't be stingy. Don't discriminate between the people you like and those you can't stand. People who use their minds like that won't be able to awaken, nor will they be able to master the use of their fundamental mind.

## How to Embrace Others

**Questioner 2 (Male)** For a long time, I've had a sense that when we are born into this world,

로 쓸 수 있으면서도 더럽혀지지 않는 그런 무한의 백지인데, 사람들은 거기에다가 그림을 그리기도 하고, 글씨를 쓰기도 하고, 술을 거르기도 하고, 심지어는 쓰레기를 버리기도 합니다.

물론 백지 자체는 무한정이고 절대 더러워질 게 없으니 훼손될 거는 없겠습니다만 막 쓰는 사람들을 보면 나는 나 스스로를 다잡으면서 '나는 잘 써야 되겠다. 나나 잘하자. 일단 나라도 올바르게 가자. 다 나를 공부시켜 주는 과정이구나!' 하고 갑니다. 그런데 내가 나를 위해서 수행하는 건 기본인 거고, 이 가르침이 어차피 전체로서 같이 가지 않을 수 없는 것이다 보니, 서로 다 잘되어야 될 거 같은 생각이 듭니다.

each one of us brings a blank sheet of paper. It's completely empty, and we can write anything we want to, and use it in any way we want. Some people write stories, others draw pictures, still others filter alcohol through it, and some people even dump their trash on it.

Of course, this paper is infinite, never stained, and can't be damaged. Yet when I see people use it recklessly, I check my own behavior, thinking, "I need to use my mind wisely. I have to get my act together. I need to go forward in the right direction." And I remind myself that everything I'm encountering is part of the process of learning and evolving. I understand that spiritual practice is necessary for my own well-being, but we also need to use it for the well-being of others because this truth of *one mind* [24] is the truth that we are all living and working together.

---

**24. One mind** (Hanmaum [han-ma-um]): From the Korean, where "one" has a nuance of great and combined, while "mind" is more than intellect and includes "heart" as well. Together, they mean everything combined and connected as one. What is called "one mind" is intangible, unseen, and transcends time and space. It has no beginning or end, and is sometimes called our fundamental mind. It also means the mind of all beings and everything in the universe connected and working together as one.

그래서 드리는 말씀인데, 나 하나 잘 살기 위해 나 하나 죽이는 거는 쉬운데, 이기적으로 막사는 사람들도 많은데 그런 걸 보면서도 같이 잘 살기 위해서 나를 죽이는 거는 참말로 어려운 것 같습니다. 그 부분에 대해서 큰스님의 가르침을 부탁드립니다.

**큰스님** 이 근본마음이라는 게요, 사실 안과 밖이 없이 그저 텅 비어서 고요하기 때문에, 아니, 사실 고요하다랄 것도 없고, 이름조차 따로 붙일 것도 없어요.

그렇게 아무런 분별이 없는 게 근본마음인데, 거기에다 내가 '나를 위해, 전체를 위해' 이런 식으로 구분 지어 놓는 게 잘못된 거지요. 그러니까 너, 나 이런 걸 구분하지 말고, 마음을 내 보세요.

그러면 그 사람을 위해 '내가 했다, 내가 한다.' 이런 걸 떠올릴 것도 없이, 서로 저절로 잘 돌아가게끔 돼 있습니다. 다시 말해 '둘이 아니게 모두가 잘 살 수 있게 된다.' 이런 뜻이에요.

So my problem is this: I can let go when it's something that benefits me, but when it's necessary for others, I have a really hard time. Can you give me some advice about how I can overcome this?

**Kun Sunim**  This fundamental mind of ours! It has no inside or outside. It's completely empty and utterly serene. Actually, we can't even use words like "serene" because all words and descriptions fail to even scratch its essence.

This fundamental mind encompasses everything, without the least discrimination, so if you're thinking about practice in terms of "for myself" or "for others," then you've gone astray. When something confronts you, and you raise and entrust an intention for that, do so while letting go of any distinctions of "you" versus "me."

If you go forward letting go of both sides like this, things will naturally work out well for you and for others, and make it possible for everyone involved to live together non-dually.

Nonetheless, you still need to pay attention to doing things wisely. For example, even though you sincerely want to help someone, if your words are likely to upset or irritate them, then don't say

그런데 지혜도 필요합니다. 예를 들어서, 누군가를 도와주고 싶은데 그 사람이 말로 하면 비뚤어질 거 같고 섭섭하게 들을 거 같으면, 말로 하지 말고 마음으로 보시를 하고, 말을 하면 받아들이거나 문을 열 거 같으면, 웃으면서 다가가 보세요. 하지만 그것도 말을 가지고 하는 게 아니라 다른 말을 하다가 슬그머니 듣게끔 하는 지혜가 있어야겠죠. 지금 사찰도 많고 공부하는 사람도 많지만, 그렇게 실천할 수 있어야만 모두 잘 살 수 있게 되겠지요.

### 원망하는 마음 바꾸기

**질문자 3(남)** 제가 일이 잘 안됐든지 할 때면, 남을 원망하는 마음이 참 많이 생깁니다. 또 남이 저를 괴롭힐 때면, 그 사람이 잘못되기를 바라는 마음도 생기고요. 법회 자리에 오거나, 큰스님 법문을 접할 때는 '이러면 안 되는데….' 하다가도 일상생활로 돌아가면 또 그럽니다. 저의 이런 마음이 좀 덜 들게 할 수 있으신지요?

anything at all. Instead, work through this fundamental mind, raising generous, harmonious intentions, and then entrust those to your foundation.

If you're talking with them and it looks like they're open to what you'd say, then that's fine. But even in that case, it's better to be a bit indirect and just nudge them. There may be lots of books about Buddhism these days, but it's only when we can put our knowledge into practice like this that our lives will begin to improve. All of our lives. All together, as one whole.

### Freeing Yourself from Resentment

**Questioner 3 (Male)** Hello, I've noticed that when things at work don't go well, I find myself really resenting the people responsible. Likewise, if someone harasses me or deliberately causes me problems, I end up wishing that something bad would happen to them. However, when I come here and listen to your Dharma talks, I realize that I shouldn't be thinking like that. Yet when Monday comes around, it starts all over again. Can you make these thoughts disappear, or at least cause them to not arise so often?

**큰스님**  그거야 내가 해줄 수 있는 게 아니죠. 하하하. 자기 끌고 다니는 운전수한테 그러세요. 사고 안 나게 잘 끌고 다니고, 기름 떨어지지 않게 잘 넣고 다니라고요. 운전수가 차를 끌고 다니는 거지, 차가 운전수를 끌로 다니는 게 아닙니다.

그런 거처럼 나를 끌고 다니는 거는 내 근본, 내 주인공입니다. 그러니 거기다 일임하세요. 만약 어떤 사람이 악한 마음을 가지고 나한테 다가오더라도 '원래 저 사람 마음과 내 마음은 둘이 아니야. 생명의 근본도 둘이 아니고, 마음 내기 이전의 마음도 둘이 아니야. 그러니 다 마음을 밝게 해서 다시 **한마음**[11]이 되게 해. 주인공! 당신만이 할 수 있어.' 하고 거기다 다 맡겨 보세요.

---

11. **한마음**: '한'이란 광대무변함, 일체가 하나로 합쳐진 것을 뜻하며, 한마음이란 만질 수도 없고 보이지도 않으며, 시공간을 초월하여, 시작도 끝도 없는 근본마음을 말함. 또한, 만물만생의 마음이 삼천대천세계와 서로 연결되어 하나로 돌아가는 것을 의미하기도 함. 다시 말해, 한마음은 우주 전체와 그 속에서 살고 있는 일체 생명들이 근본을 통해 서로 연결되어 그 마음들이 하나로 돌아가는 모든 작용을 포함하고 있음.

**Kun Sunim** [Laughs.] No one else can do that for you. The person who can take care of that is the one you see in the mirror every day. That's who moves your body and makes things happen. Your car doesn't drive itself, right? It's the driver who checks the oil and gas, and works at avoiding accidents.

Just like this, it's your foundation, your Juingong, that moves and directs you. So entrust everything there. Even if someone approaches you with evil intent, completely entrust that to your foundation, thinking, "Inherently his mind and my mind are connected. The foundation of all life is one, and this mind that exists before any thoughts arose is also one. So, true self, Juingong, brighten this light within him and make our minds one again." Know that your foundation is taking care of this, and completely entrust everything.

Let go of hatred and resentment. Just entrust all of that to your foundation and live peacefully. The fact is, your opinions, judgements, and perceptions keep you from seeing the whole. They prevent you from understanding what's really going on. So don't get caught up in thoughts like "He ruined

증오심을 버리시고요. 그런 것도 내 근본자리에다 맡기시고, 그냥 편안하게 대하세요. 잘 알지도 못하면서 자기 사량으로 상대방이 날 망하게 했다고 생각한다거나 하면 안 돼요. 사람과의 관계에서 불편한 일이 생기면 쓸데없이 이리저리 생각하지 말고, 그냥 내 근본에 맡기세요.

상대방의 말이나 행동이 설사 나를 해하려고 하는 거라도, 이게 되레 나를 더 잘되게 만들 수도 있는 거고, 또 내가 지레짐작으로 오해할 수도 있는 겁니다.

그러니 복잡하게 사량심을 낼 게 아니라, '주인공, 모두를 의합하게 하여 같이 불이 들어오게 해. 그래서 다 같이 밝은 데서 살게끔 해. 당신만이 그렇게 할 수 있어.' 라고 하면서 맡기세요. 그러면 상대방 가슴에 불이 들어와서 댁의 마음과 하나가 될 수 있습니다. 자기가 잘못된 게 있으면 사과도 하고요. 이런 게 서로가 친절해질 수 있는 방법이지요.

my life." As you work at your ordinary, daily life, when you have some conflicts or problems with people, don't worry or obsess over those. That's useless. Just entrust all of it to your foundation. Even if it seems like someone is trying to harm or slander you, entrust that as well.

Even though they had bad intent, that situation could turn into something good for you in the end. Or it may be the case that you misunderstood their actions entirely.

So don't get caught up in your opinions and judgements, nor in replaying the situation over and over. Just entrust the whole thing to your foundation, knowing, "Juingong! Let's all live together harmoniously, and allow the inner light we all have to become brighter." Know that your foundation is what can make all of this happen. Then, the other person's mind will become brighter, and your relationships can become more harmonious. And if one of you did something wrong, you may become aware of it and apologize. This is how you can become warmer towards each other.

**질문자 4(남)**  살면서 회향(回向)하는 것에 대해 말씀 올리고자 합니다.

고난과 액난이 나를 공부시키는 재료라 해도, 그런 일들이 생기길 바라는 분들은 아무도 없을 겁니다. 사실, 관(觀)하는 과정에서 고난이나 액난이 그냥 사라져 주길 바라는 마음이 대부분이죠.

그리고 그 과정에서 혹시 좋게 일이 잘되면 감사하게 회향을 잘합니다. 하지만 막상 고난과 액난이 지속되면 당황하게 되고 어쩔 줄을 모르는 경우가 많습니다.

### Giving Back and How to Finish Things Up Well

**Questioner 4 (Male)**  I'd like to ask you about the idea of "giving back" when we've finished something.[25]

When something finishes or some problem works itself out, we often try to give something back to others, knowing that's an important part of finishing things well. People often sense that what we share with others ends up helping us.

Although hardships and difficulties can cause us to grow, no one actually wants them. In fact, it seems that for a lot of people, when they say they're entrusting those problems, they're actually just trying to wish them away.

Anyway, although we try to give back at the end of something, what about the case where suffering never seems to finish? People often seem to lose their hope and focus when hardships go on and on.

---

**25.** Literally, "returning back" (回向). In Korean Buddhism, this implies the practice of giving back or sharing with others at the successful conclusion of something. While it's understood that this is a good thing to do, and will also benefit oneself and one's ancestors, it doesn't have the strong nuance of "transferring merit to one's ancestors" that it has in Chinese Buddhism.

제 생각에는 원해서 온 거는 아니지만, 어찌 됐든 고난이나 액난이 오면 어차피 겪어야 될 일이니 '이건 공부의 재료고 스승이다. 스승님이 나를 가르쳐 주러 오셨다.' 하는 생각을 내는 게 좋을 것 같습니다. 그런 감사하는 마음을 가진다면 오히려 그 경계가 하나의 회향할 수 있는 여지가 되지 않을까 하는 생각도 들고요.

그런 자세가 되어야 고난을 적극적으로 견뎌낼 수 있고, 이길 수 있고, 또 거기서 정말 한소식 들을 수 있는 그러한 자리가 생기지 않을까 하는 생각이 듭니다. 그래서 회향을 좋고 감사할 때만 할 것이 아니라, 오히려 어려울 때, 힘들 때 하는 그 회향이 더욱 큰 정진의 거름이 될 것 같다 하는 생각에서 말씀을 드립니다.

**큰스님** 그런데요, 사람들 인생이 천차만별이다 보니 회향도 천차만별로 합니다. 하지만 방법은 달라도 중요한 건 어떻게 마무리를 잘 짓고 가느냐죠. 잘 마무리를 지으며 가야 회향을 잘하고 가는 거거든요.

It seems to me that it's better to view and accept the hardships we face as something that has come to teach us. Even though those are not something we want, we still have to face them, so if we take them as a chance to learn, we can get through them a little easier. The act of viewing things positively like this feels like it becomes energy that feeds and sustains my practice.

That energy helps me face my suffering and overcome it, and will perhaps even lead me to awakening. So it seems to me that "giving back" isn't for the end, when something's finished, but rather, it's what we should do even while in the middle of our suffering. Am I understanding this correctly?

**Kun Sunim**   You're not wrong, but people's lives are very different, so how they give back and how they view what confronts them are likewise very different. Although they think of all this in different ways, the important point is finishing things up well. If you can do this, that giving back will be taken care of as well.

예를 들어서, 허구한 날 술을 마시고, 집안을 난가를 만들면서 인생을 마칠 수도 있고, 또는 두세 살림을 차려가며 살다가 가족끼리 서로 은혈이 지게끔 해놓고 갈 수도 있고, 수수하게 잘 살다가 그냥 갈 수도 있고, 아니면 적극적으로 내가 뿌린 씨는 내가 거둔다는 그러한 일념으로 살다 갈 수도 있겠죠.

그런데 이런 공부를 하는 스님네들은 일체 회향을 합니다. 일체 회향은 우리가 살면서 매 순간 일체를 내 근본에 돌려놓아 모든 걸 회향하는 걸 말합니다. 그렇기 때문에 죽고 나서의 회향은 없습니다.

살아 있는 동안 모든 걸 내 근본에 돌려놓으면 삼세가 하나로 돌아가기에 다시 태어나고 죽고 하는 윤회의 고리에서 벗어나는 겁니다.

그래서 죽은 뒤에 열반이라고 하는 것이 아니라, 살아서 열반이 되는 겁니다.

For example, you could finish your life drinking every day and leave your family in chaos. You could cheat on your wife, leaving girlfriends and other children behind, with all of them at each other's throats. Or you could finish up leading a quiet, simple life. Or you could finish up while being deeply aware that you will end up reaping what you are sowing now.

But those people who are determined to awaken work on returning every single thing every moment while they are alive. This isn't something you can do after you're dead.

Inherently, within this fundamental mind the past, present, and future function as one whole, so if, while alive, you return everything there, then those will melt down, and you'll be able to move beyond the chains of *samsara*[26] and its ceaseless cycle of rebirth and death.

This is why I'm always telling you that nirvana has to be attained while you're alive. It's not something that falls out of the sky after you're dead.

---

**26. Samsara:** The ceaseless cycle of birth and death that all living things are continuously passing through.

시공간을 초월해 찰나찰나 나투면서, 우주와 이 대천세계를 보고 듣고 행하는 자유권을 얻는다 이런 겁니다. 이것을 가지고 부처님께서 "끝없는 바다 가운데서 도장을 받았다. **해인**(海印)**¹²**을 받았다."라고 하신 겁니다.

죽어서는 부딪힘이 없기 때문에 이 대의의 공부를, 죽고 사는 생사를 다 끊을 만큼 해야 되는 이 공부를 못 합니다. 몸이 없기 때문에 고(苦)도 없고 낙(樂)도 없어서, 공부가 되질 않죠. 이런 부딪힘이 있어야 자기를 다스리기 위해 공부가 되는 거지, 그런 게 없으면 공부가 어떻게 되겠습니까? 그러니까 죽기 전에 열반의 경지에 들어서 생사를 초월해야 됩니다. 생사를 초월해 버리면 "부처님이 나오셨다, 가셨다." 이런 말도 성사가 안 됩니다.

---

12. **해인**(海印): 큰 바다가 일체 만물을 있는 그대로 드러내 비추어 주듯이, 우주의 모든 만물이 돌아가는 이치를 깨달아 아는 부처의 지혜를 뜻함.

I'm talking about the kind of freedom that will allow you to manifest in any time or place, and endow you with the right and ability to hear, see, and act throughout the Universe and *Dharma realm*.[27] This is what the Buddha meant when he said, "Dwelling in this vast sea of wisdom, you have received the *Ocean Seal*."[28]

When you're dead, nothing impinges upon you, either good or bad, so there's nothing to work with and no chance to hone your mind or spiritual ability. You have no chance to awaken to the great meaning, which was the whole purpose of being born as a human being in the first place.

---

**27. Dharma realm** (法界): The level of reality where everything functions as an interpenetrated and connected whole. Daehaeng Kun Sunim said that this can also be called the Dharma Net and compared it to our circulatory system, which connects and nourishes every single cell in the body.

**28. Ocean Seal** (海印): This term has a number of nuances, the most common of which is having, without a doubt (as if stamped with a seal), attained the state where the functioning of everything is perceived clearly and truly, like images seen on calm water. It includes, as well, the nuance of horizons without end and depths that cannot be measured.

그래서 일체 회향이란 살아생전에 근본자리에 모든 걸 놓는 겁니다. 일체지(一切智)에 회향한다는 건 그런 뜻입니다. 그렇기에 살면서 모든 걸 회향을 한다고 하는 것도 깨달음에 이르는 하나의 방편입니다.

회향을 간단하게 설명하자면, 예를 들어 '내가 애들을 데리고 나갔으면 집에까지 데려다 놓는다.' 이런 겁니다. 바깥에 그냥 놓지 말고 안에다가 데려다 놓는 게 회향입니다.

Through this practice of knowing your fundamental mind, you can be free across all realms and states of living and dying, but you need a body to get to this point. There have to be things confronting you in order for you to develop wisdom. You have to be able to observe how your fundamental mind works with those obstacles. So this is why I'm always telling you that you have to attain nirvana while you're alive in order to shatter the chains of samsara.

Once you've transcended life and death, you realize that saying things like "the Buddha appeared," or, "the Buddha left," is just so much nonsense.

Thus, when you return absolutely everything to your foundation like this, you are truly "finishing things up well," and "giving back." This is why it's said that "giving back" is one of the paths to awakening.

To put it another way, if you take your children out, you should bring them home. Leaving the kids outside is not "finishing things up well," nor is it "giving back."

그러니까 애당초에 자기 능력 밖의 일을 맡아서 해주겠다 하지 마세요. 자기가 자기 분수를 알고, 내가 갖고 있는 능력 내에서 일하고, 끝을 잘 마치세요. 그게 회향입니다.

자기 분수를 모르고 들뜬 마음으로 그냥 인생살이를 하는 사람들은 자기가 뿌린 걸 제대로 마무리 짓지 못하고 끝을 마치는 경우가 많아요. 그러면 회향이 제대로 안 된 겁니다. 회향이 따로 있는 게 아니라 인생을 살면서 찰나찰나 잘 마무리 지으면서 가는 게 회향이에요.

그러니까 우리가 부담스럽게 살 필요는 없어요. 그저 진실하게 '내가 뿌린 거 내가 거둔다.' 하는 생각으로 사시면 돼요. '나는 절대로 양심을 속이지 않는다. 속인다.' 이런 것도 필요 없어요. 그냥 남을 나와 같이 생각하고 또 남의 아픔을 내 아픔같이 생각하되, 자기 분수를 알고 주위에 피해를 주지 않고 조화롭게 살라는 겁니다.

So don't tell people you'll take care of something that's beyond your ability. Know your own capacity. Work within your ability and leave things neatly wrapped up. This is how you give back.

People who tend to be reckless and irresponsible leave behind messes they can't take care of. They leave behind all kinds of loose ends. There's nothing about their lives that's wrapped up well. "Finishing things up well" and "giving back" are nothing other than taking good care of each thing as it arises in your life.

There's no need to be overwhelmed by this. If you live with the awareness that "I will reap what I sow," that's enough. This is easier than you think. There's no need for complicated oaths or vows – just view others as yourself. Think of their pain as your own pain. Try to know the limits of your own ability, have a realistic view of your place in the world, don't cause harm to others, and live together harmoniously.

예를 들어 자기 처지는 생각 안 하고, 큰돈을 빌려주거나, 의리를 지킨답시고 보증을 서 주거나, 큰돈을 빌려주거나 해버리면 본인은 물론 가족들도 힘들게 될 수 있어요.

그런 건 상대방이 안 갚아도 내가 그걸 다 감당해 낼 능력이 됐을 때, 해주는 겁니다. 겨우 집 한 채 있고, 땅 몇 뙈기 있다고 보증을 선다거나 해버리면, 자기 자신은 말할 것도 없고, 식구들까지도 거지 만들어 놓을 수가 있어요.

이러는 건 회향이 아닙니다. 착하기만 한 게 부처님의 가르침이 아니며, 또 그렇게 하는 게 착한 것도 아니에요. 착하게 사는 건 그런 게 아니에요. 똑똑하고 착한 건 따로 있습니다. 석가모니 부처님은 그렇게 희미하게 살라고 가르치지 않으셨어요. 양면을 다 일러 주셨습니다.

For example, some people will lend money or sign loan guarantees out of a sense of loyalty or duty, but without reflecting upon their own circumstances. Although they meant well, they can end up causing horrible problems for their own family.

If you have enough money that you won't be bothered if a loan is never repaid, then go ahead and lend it if you want to. But when all you have is a house and a small plot of farmland, you have no business doing things that could cause your family to end up living under a bridge.

In no way whatsoever is lending money or signing a loan guarantee in these circumstances "giving back." Just being kind and good isn't what the Buddha taught. Not to mention the fact that signing those kinds of documents isn't actually a good or kind thing to do. There's neither wisdom nor kindness there. Leaving that sort of mess behind isn't what Sakyamuni Buddha taught. He taught us to be wise as well as kind. He showed how we can develop the wisdom and ability to truly benefit both others and ourselves. You've

불, 법, 승의 의미를 깊이 한번 새겨 보십시오. 깊이 새겨 보고 정확하고 똑똑하면서도 인자하고 둥글게 사십시오.

all heard of the *Buddha, Dharma, and Sangha*,[29] right?

Well, "Buddha" means the great, interconnected power and essential nature of our foundation. "Dharma" is a thought or intention arising from this, and "Sangha" is that thought and energy manifesting and functioning in the material world.

Think deeply about this and the implications it has for your own life, and live wisely, generously, and harmoniously.

---

**29. Buddha, Dharma, and Sangha:** Outwardly, these are Sakyamuni Buddha, his teachings about the truth, and the community of practitioners and the faithful. In this example, Daehaeng Kun Sunim is explaining their inner aspects.

# 한마음출판사의 마음을 밝혀 주는 도서

# 해외출판사에서 출판된 한마음도서

- Wake Up And Laugh
  Wisdom Publications, 미국

- No River To Cross
  (*No River To Cross, No Raft To Find* 영어판)
  Wisdom Publications, 미국

- Wie Fließendes Wasser
  (*My Heart Is A Golden Buddha* 독일어판)
  Goldmann Arkana-Random House, 독일

- Wie Fließendes Wasser - CD
  (*My Heart Is A Golden Buddha* 독일어판 오디오북)
  steinbach sprechende bücher

- Ningún Río Que Cruzar
  (*No River To Cross* 스페인어판)
  Kailas Editorial, S.L., 스페인

- Umarmt Von Mitgefühl
  ('만가지 꽃이 피고 만가지 열매 익어':
  대행큰스님의 뜻으로 푼 천수경 독일어판)
  Diederichs-Random House, 독일

- 我心是金佛
  (*My Heart Is A Golden Buddha* 번체자 중국어판)
  橡樹林文化出版, 대만

- Vertraue Und Lass Alles Los
  (*No River To Cross* 독일어판)
  Goldmann Arkana-Random House, 독일

- Wache Auf Und Lache
  (*Wake Up And Laugh* 독일어판)
  Theseus, 독일

• Дзэн И Просветление
（No River To Cross 러시아어판）
Amrita-Rus, 러시아

• Sup Cacing Tanah
（*My Heart Is A Golden Buddha* 인도네시아어판）
PT Gramedia, 인도네시아

• Không có sông nào để vượt qua
（*No River To Cross* 베트남어판）
Vien Chieu, 베트남

• Probuď se!
(*Wake Up And Laugh* 체코어판)
(Eugenika, 체코)

• tỉnh thức và cười
(*Wake Up And Laugh* 베트남어판)
Vien Chieu, 베트남

## Other Books by Seon Master Daehaeng

**English**
- Wake Up And Laugh (Wisdom Publications)
- No River To Cross (Wisdom Publications)
- My Heart Is A Golden Buddha (Hanmaum Publications)
  *Also available as an audiobook*
- Standing Again (Hanmaum Publications)
- Sharing the Same Heart (Hanmaum Publications)
- Touching The Earth (Hanmaum Publications)
- A Thousand Hands of Compassion
  (Hanmaum Publications) [Korean/English]
- One Mind: Principles (Hanmaum Publications)
  *★All of these are available in paper or ebook formats*

- Practice in Daily Life (Korean/English bilingual series)
  1. To Discover Your True Self, "I" Must Die
  2. Walking Without A Trace
  3. Let Go And Observe
  4. Mind, Treasure House Of Happiness
  5. The Furnace Within Yourself
  6. The Spark That Can Save The Universe
  7. The Infinite Power Of One Mind
  8. In The Heart of A Moment
  9. One With The Universe
  10. Protecting The Earth
  11. Inherent Connections
  12. Finding A Way Forward
  13. Faith In Action
  14. The Healing Power of Our Inner Light
  15. The Doctor Is In
  16. Turning Dirt Into Gold
  17. Dancing on the Whirlwind

**Korean**
- 건널 강이 어디 있으랴 (Hanmaum Publications)
- 내 마음은 금부처 (Hanmaum Publications)
- 처음 시작하는 마음공부1 (Hanmaum Publications)

**Russian**
- Дзэн И Просветление (Amrita-Rus)

**German**
- Wache Auf und Lache (Theseus)
- Umarmt von Mitgefühl (Deutsch·Koreanisch, Diederichs)
- Wie fließendes Wasser (Goldmann)
- Wie fließendes Wasser - CD (steinbach sprechende bücher)
- Vertraue und lass alles los (Goldmann)
- Grundlagen (Hanmaum Publications)

**Czech**
- Probuď se! (Eugenika)

**Spanish**
- Ningún Río Que Cruzar (Kailas Editorial)
- Una Semilla Inherente Alimenta El Universo
  (Hanmaum Publications)
- Si Te Lo Propones, No Hay Imposibles
  (Hanmaum Publications)
- El Camino Interior (Hanmaum Publications)
- Vida De La Maestra Seon Daehaeng
  (Hanmaum Publications)
- Enseñanzas De La Maestra Daehaeng
  (Hanmaum Publications)

**Indonesian**
- Sup Cacing Tanah (PT Gramedia)

**Vietnamese**
- Không có sông nào để vượt qua
  (Hanmaum Publications; Vien Chieu, Vietnam)
- tinh thức và cưới
  (Hanmaum Publications; Vien Chieu, Vietnam)

**Chinese**
- 我心是金佛〔简体字〕(Hanmaum Publications, 韩国)
- 无河可渡〔简体字〕(Hanmaum Publications, 韩国)
- 人生不是苦海〔繁体字〕(Hanmaum Publications, 韩国)
- 我心是金佛〔繁体字〕(橡树林文化出版, 台湾)

# 한마음선원본원

경기도 안양시 만안구 경수대로 1282 (석수동, 한마음선원)
(우) 13908
Tel : 82-31-470-3100   Fax : 82-31-470-3116
홈페이지 : http://www.hanmaum.org
이메일 : jongmuso@hanmaum.org


# 국내지원

**강릉지원** (우)25565 강원도 강릉시 하평5길 29 (포남동)
　　　　　 TEL:(033) 651-3003   FAX:(033) 652-0281

**공주지원** (우)32522 충청남도 공주시 사곡면 위안양골길 157-61
　　　　　 TEL:(041) 852-9100   FAX:(041) 852-9105

**광명선원** (우)27638 충청북도 음성군 금왕읍 대금로 1402
　　　　　 TEL:(043) 877-5000   FAX:(043) 877-2900

**광주지원** (우)61965 광주광역시 서구 운천로 204번길 23-1 (치평동)
　　　　　 TEL:(062) 373-8801   FAX:(062) 373-0174

**대구지원** (우)42152 대구광역시 수성구 수성로 41길 76 (중동)
　　　　　 TEL:(053) 767-3100   FAX:(053) 765-1600

**목포지원** (우)58696 전라남도 목포시 백년대로 266번길 31-1 (상동)
　　　　　 TEL:(061) 284-1771   FAX:(061) 284-1770

**문경지원** (우)36937 경상북도 문경시 산양면 봉서1길 10
　　　　　 TEL:(054) 555-8871   FAX:(054) 556-1989

**부산지원** (우)49113 부산광역시 영도구 함지로 79번길 23-26 (동삼동)
　　　　　 TEL:(051) 403-7077   FAX:(051) 403-1077

**울산지원** (우)44200 울산광역시 북구 달래골길 26-12 (천곡동)
　　　　　 TEL:(052) 295-2335   FAX:(052) 295-2336

**제주지원** (우)63308 제주특별자치도 제주시 황사평6길 176-1 (영평동)
TEL:(064) 727-3100   FAX:(064) 727-0302

**중부경남** (우)50871 경상남도 김해시 진영읍 하계로35
TEL:(055) 345-9900   FAX:(055) 346-2179

**진주지원** (우)52602 경상남도 진주시 미천면 오방로 528-40
TEL:(055) 746-8163   FAX:(055) 746-7825

**청주지원** (우)28540 충청북도 청주시 청원구 교서로 109
TEL:(043) 259-5599   FAX:(043) 255-5599

**통영지원** (우)53021 경상남도 통영시 광도면 조암길 45-230
TEL:(055) 643-0643   FAX:(055) 643-0642

**포항지원** (우)37635 경상북도 포항시 북구 우창로 59 (우현동)
TEL:(054) 232-3163   FAX:(054) 241-3503

## Anyang Headquarters of Hanmaum Seonwon

1282 Gyeongsu-daero, Manan-gu, Anyang-si,
Gyeonggi-do, 13908, Republic of Korea
Tel: (82-31) 470-3175 / Fax: (82-31) 470-3209
www.hanmaum.org/eng
onemind@hanmaum.org


## Overseas Branches of Hanmaum Seonwon

**ARGENTINA**
Buenos Aires
Miró 1575, CABA, C1406CVE, Rep. Argentina
Tel: (54-11) 4921-9286 / Fax: (54-11) 4921-9286
http://hanmaumbsas.org

Tucumán
Av. Aconquija 5250, El Corte, Yerba Buena,
Tucumán, T4107CHN, Rep. Argentina
Tel: (54-381) 425-1400
www.hanmaumtuc.org

**BRASIL**
São Paulo
R. Newton Prado 540, Bom Retiro
Sao Paulo, CEP 01127-000, Brasil
Tel: (55-11) 3337-5291
www.hanmaumbr.org

**CANADA**
Toronto
20 Mobile Dr., North York, Ontario M4A 1H9, Canada
Tel: (1-416) 750-7943
www.hanmaum.org/toronto

**GERMANY**
Kaarst
Broicherdorf Str. 102, 41564 Kaarst, Germany
Tel: (49-2131) 969551 / Fax: (49-2131) 969552
www.hanmaum-zen.de

**THAILAND**
Bangkok
86/1 Soi 4 Ekamai Sukhumvit 63
Bangkok, Thailand
Tel: (66-2) 391-0091
www.hanmaum.org/cafe/thaihanmaum

**USA**
Chicago
7852 N. Lincoln Ave., Skokie, IL 60077, USA
Tel: (1-847) 674-0811
www.hanmaum.org/chicago

Los Angeles
1905 S. Victoria Ave., L.A., CA 90016, USA
Tel: (1-323) 766-1316
www.hanmaum.org/la

New York
144-39, 32 Ave., Flushing, NY 11354, USA
Tel: (1-718) 460-2019 / Fax: (1-718) 939-3974
www.juingong.org

Washington D.C.
7807 Trammel Rd., Annandale, VA 22003, USA
Tel: (1-703) 560-5166
www.hanmaum.org/wa

책에 관한 문의나 주문을 하실 분들은
아래의 연락처로 문의해 주십시오.

**한마음국제문화원/한마음출판사**
경기도 안양시 만안구 경수대로 1282 ㈜13908
전화: (82-31) 470-3175
팩스: (82-31) 470-3209
e-mail: onemind@hanmaum.org
hanmaumbooks.org

If you would like more information about these books
or would like to order copies of them,
please call or write to:

**Hanmaum International Culture Institute
Hanmaum Publications**
1282 Gyeongsu-daero, Manan-gu, Anyang-si,
Gyeonggi-do, 13908,
Republic of Korea
Tel: (82-31) 470-3175
Fax: (82-31) 470-3209
e-mail: onemind@hanmaum.org
hanmaumbooks.org